TANGO

SEX AND RHYTHM OF THE CITY

MIKE GONZALEZ AND
MARIANELLA YANES

REAKTION BOOKS

With thanks to Antonio, my father, who loved Gardel; Elena and Candelario for the tangos that you sang; Benito Velasco, for his tango club in Caracas.

Published by Reaktion Books Ltd
33 Great Sutton Street
London EC1V 0DX, UK
www.reaktionbooks.co.uk

First published 2013

Printed and bound in Great Britain
by Bell & Bain, Glasgow

A catalogue record for this book is available from the British Library.
ISBN 9 781 78023 107 5

CONTENTS

PROLOGUES

TANGO MINE: MARIANELLA'S STORY

My home in Caracas was a place of peace at a turbulent political time, perhaps because it was a temple of women, to which men were invited at weekends. My sisters and I, the spoiled children of my nine aunts who shared our weekends and its endless meals, mimicked in our small way the steps and the lyrics that emerged from the vinyl records spinning on the record player. The music was a mix of popular ballads, rancheras, son and mambos – all very useful when the time came to polish the floor in preparation for an evening's dancing. In those days the floors were polished with hot wax dissolved in paraffin, a process so dangerous that the children had to be kept out of the room until the concrete floor tiles were covered. Then we were allowed in to help with the polishing by dancing on spongy rags tied to our feet – floor polishers were an unimaginable luxury. The job was done only when those coloured floors were glassy enough to reflect our faces in them. And we all sang while we danced. We could guess the mood of my mother, my grandmother, our neighbours and our wonderful aunts who accompanied us throughout our childhood, from the rhythm of the music. Disappointment in love, betrayal and rejection found some consolation only in the tango, the rancheras and the popular ballads. And that became even more intense and interesting when the television was turned on to watch the Dark Skinned Boy From Abasto, dear Carlos Gardel, in those melodramatic performances with which he graced Argentine cinema in the early Thirties. My aunts wept, my mother sighed – she was never one for tears, like my grandmother, whose hard exterior softened only with that seductive suffering look that Gardel wore when he sang 'Her eyes closed'. And my grandmother would say, 'How sad, the poor man, alone without his mother – and men without mothers always suffer!' It was a hint directed at my mother because she couldn't cook and had divorced and because her second marriage, from which my sisters were born, had not been blessed in church. My grandmother's criticisms were merciless, even though the situation was common to most working-class Latin American families. In general, couples got together without the approval of the Church or the civil registry; my grandmother herself was an example, with her three couplings, each of which had produced a child. Still, she did not expect her children to repeat her life story and the tango songs offered faithful portraits of her world.

But the big event of the weekend began after lunch, when the lovers appeared with their guitars to sing their passionate serenades, just like the lovers in Mexican films who sang beneath the balconies of their beloveds. The songs – tangos, boleros and rancheras – sounded authentic in their mouths, turning their dramatic lyrics into declarations of love that in that feminine space fertilized the unions and the separations of the future. There were the sisters in love with the same man, the men seducing several of the sisters, the bedroom secrets, the unexpected pregnancies, the jealousies, flirtations and rejections that only alcohol or new secret passions could assuage.

There, surrounded by the seductive dances and the melodious strumming of guitars, I learned the melodramatic visions that each tango contained. I absorbed them so well that their tragic vision of the world became words in the dialogues between the actors in the soap operas that I wrote for Venezuelan television.

Tango is more than a tuneful entertainment: it is a portrait of poor men and women, it is a sharp prick of hunger and thirst, it is a desolate road to homes overwhelmed by need. But at the same time, it is the undefined pleasure of the forbidden. The solitude of a prostitute's empty room, the absence of love, the warmth of a Sunday family dinner, the things you left behind and the things you never achieved. The loss of a mother – that miraculous woman who would embrace you and expect only a brief kiss in return. The hardest thing was that the tango left us with a feeling of the loss of a country, of rootlessness, of the absence of that sense of belonging that tango reflected. And it expressed the need to construct and create a new life out of nothing. Hence *lunfardo*, the special language of tango. I reinvent language in order to belong, but I base this new language on what I have forgotten in order to become what I am. It is a language of immediate reference; it speaks of the immigrant's life in poverty.

These were the lyrics, the music and the violent and seductive steps of the tango. It is a temptation to dance tango, but not the kind of temptation that drags you to the dance floor to try it and see. Every movement, every gesture, every encounter demands preparation. Like lunfardo, the tango has to be learned over time. Its syncopated notes draw you in, absorb you, but learning its rhythm is the vital condition for the encounter. It is like an adolescent's initiation into adult life. First you listen to the music and let it seduce you. Before you dance, you learn how to dress for the milonga – the dance. For women: silk stockings, a garter belt, a skirt split on one side or in the middle. A low neckline. A flower in the hair and finally, high-heeled shoes. That is what seduces; it is a kind of fetish, with the long heel stroking the partner's leg. It is the smallest of gestures, a momentary touch, barely a caress to inspire those three minutes called 'Tango'. The man has his ritual too. The hat, the suit, the penetrating smell of lavender and perfume, the carnation or the violet in the lapel, the two-toned shoes with a small heel pointing forward. All these components gathered on the dance floor, in a ritual of pain, death, and the anguish of love and rejection, all in a ritual of despair that ends in that final embrace – the meeting and the farewell called 'tango'.

THE DANCERS

It is an elegant shoe: high-heeled, and in gleaming patent leather crowned by a spat that holds the smooth black trouser leg. It lifts slightly, points forward and down, then slides along the floor, brushing against her fine black stocking. Her foot, resting back on spiked heels, arched and naked, lifts and responds in kind. Later, left foot follows right, now twisting, now engaging, now trapping her legs between his. The split skirt lets her respond, entwine and unravel, pirouette, a stroking capture of leg and thigh, hers open and suggestive, his dark and constrained by the tight-fitting suit.

The music is dramatic, fast, punctuated by sudden accents and shrill curls of violin and bandoneon. The narrative is a rhythm of lunge and counter, invitation and rejection. From the waist down, these restless bodies seek each other out in a ceaseless pursuit. Yet the upper body tells a different story. He leans over her at a constant angle, pushing and demanding, his back taut and unyielding; she bends slightly back, in an attitude of surrender. It does not seem to fit the sensuous encounter of legs and feet, so intimate, so full of desire.

Most perplexing are the eyes – the look, or rather its absence. There is neither challenge nor defiance, no dare and counter-dare. The engagement of the bodies is matched by a disengagement of the face. The dancers look at each other yet also beyond and into the distance; all that is here is indifference, a refusal to connect as resolute as the endless brushing of legs and thighs.

This is the paradox of tango.

1 STRANGERS IN THE CITY

Behind the grand domes and palaces of Genoa, I could see the mountains still. Apricale wasn't far away, just there, behind that second hill, where that tree is bending slightly in the wind. I grew up there, in dark cobbled streets with hundreds of corners and crannies where we could hide and play, along with the cats. There must have been a million cats in the village. You looked up and it seemed as if God had opened his hands and dropped the houses onto the hilltop and that they had tumbled down and stopped at crazy angles. We had our fields, my dad and I, up above the village, looking down. Some mornings you could hardly breathe when you got up there, particularly on winter mornings, when the wind was cold and the sun froze you in its light. But when my dad died, things changed.

The ship is moving now. I can hardly see. There are so many of us on deck watching, weeping, blinking so that the image of those mountains stays printed on the inside of our eyelids and we can take it with us to where we're going. Wherever that is. That man on the foredeck with the captain, the one in the frock coat and the top hat with a blue and white sash, he knows. He's the one who found us, who told us that on the other side of the world was a country waiting for us. There was land there. There were empty farms with houses that we could live in – the keys were above the door, ready for us. It was so vast, this place, that we would have to board a train and travel a day and a night. But

> first they would give us a room in a hotel, and food. And they would welcome us.
>
> I can hardly see my hills now. I can see Genoa, disappearing into the mist. Everyone is crying now, waving – but who to? Who knows how long it will be before we come back here, to Liguria. Perhaps we will come back with new families, and perhaps we will travel in the cabins, with the gentlemen. Perhaps?

IMMIGRANTS

In 1869, Buenos Aires had 223,000 inhabitants. A single generation later, in 1914, it was the largest city in the hemisphere after New York, with a population of just over 2 million. Most dramatically, nearly 48 per cent of the city's inhabitants were foreign born. Buenos Aires had been transformed in these few years 'from a riverside town to a modern metropolis'.[1]

The city had not only changed in size in those years; it had become profoundly cosmopolitan, diverse, home to a variety of languages and cultures. And at the same time, a yawning gulf had opened up between the old city centre and the wealthy suburbs, with their elegant, well-heeled residents, and the districts around the expanding port. Here was the melting pot in which the new city was being forged.

Who were these new arrivals, these builders of the new Buenos Aires? And why had they been encouraged to come?

By the mid-1860s, the conflict that had divided Argentina since it declared independence from Spain in 1816 had been resolved. The debate about the future of the newly independent republic centred on one question. Would the country develop through its trade with the rest of Latin America, diversifying its economy as it went; or would it throw in its lot with the foreign traders (particularly the British) and grow by exporting its meat and agricultural products, exchanging them for consumer goods and manufactures imported from Europe? Each alternative carried its own political programme and its own ideology. In one case, the logic pointed in the direction of Latin American cooperation and unity, a kind of continental nationalism. In the other, Argentina would continue to be dependent on European colonial powers, and prosper as a result of that relationship.[2]

The then President of Argentina, Bartolome Mitre, a member of the wealthy landowning aristocracy whose large estates produced the goods to be exported, threw open the doors of the Argentine economy and invited foreign, but especially British investors, to put their money into the expanding meat and cereal production of his country. They took up the opportunity enthusiastically and the country moved into a new chapter in its history. The market for Argentine mutton and lamb, and its wheat, grew dramatically.

Had the plan to connect with Latin America borne fruit, the centre of the country might have been established elsewhere, in the wealthy area of Corrientes, for example. But the focus on European trade carried with it one inevitable consequence: Buenos Aires would become the heart of an independent Argentina, its port the crossroads through which all commerce passed.

And there was another expression of the triumph of the European connection; a dominant idea that progress would only be possible with the adoption of European ideas, values and behaviours – in a word, European 'civilization'. In the 1840s, two writers had given form to this view. Alberdi's slogan 'To civilize is to populate' became a kind of watchword. And the literary representation of that idea came in the form of a book, part novel part sociological treatise, written by a vigorous advocate of the European connection: Domingo Faustino Sarmiento, *Facundo* (1845) recounted the life of one of the more notorious local chieftains on the vast Argentine prairies, the *pampas*.[3] He was represented as a kind of primitive, driven solely by instinct and expressing the realities of a violent world without moral or social values. Oh, they were fine horsemen, these cowboys or *gauchos*, who followed their horses and cattle back and forth across the Argentine *pampas*. And they were free, in the way that wild animals are free. But theirs was a natural instinct that had to be tamed, if Argentina was to become the civilized nation Sarmiento and his circle imagined. Natural man must be replaced by civilized man. In another sense, Latin American man – so close to the world of instinct and so far from the social skills indispensable for the new Argentina – had to be re-educated, forcibly if necessary. And it was not only a matter of dealing with particular individuals and their characteristics, but of eliminating the way of life which, in Sarmiento's view, inevitably produced and reproduced the Facundos of Argentine history.

In practice, this connected perfectly with the enclosure of the *pampas*, which until then were common lands grazed freely by the independent *gauchos* who moved with their herds. With their disappearance, the *pampas* could be fenced and divided into the great estates (or *estancias*) which would increasingly be devoted to producing the rich red beef for which Argentina would become justly renowned.[4]

The necessity for immigrant labour had already been antici-pated in the 1852 Constitution, that set out a surprisingly liberal policy on immigration to the new Argentina:

> The Federal Government will encourage European immigra-tion, and it will not restrict, limit or burden with any taxes the entrance into Argentine territory of foreigners who come with the goal of working the land, improving the industries and teach the sciences and the arts.

But the fact that this was more than a question of expanding the labour market is signalled in the second part of this clause. For these were immigrants who would come 'to improve and to

A gaucho cartoon.

teach'. In other words, they were already seen as the physical embodiment, the bearers of that European civilization which would transform and modernize Argentina in a single generation.

Mitre had already invited European investors to collaborate in national development in the 1850s. Now, in the late 1860s, the invitation was extended, actively, to Europe's peasant farmers and workers. And the city that would receive them, the riverside town that was fast becoming a capital city and a major port – Buenos Aires – made ready to receive them.

It is unclear whether the governments of the day had thought through how the immigrant population would live, especially given the scale of the process. Perhaps they envisaged an effortless absorption. In any event, the self-confidence of Argentina's wealthy classes was at its height as the immigrant ships arrived in numbers in the early 1870s. The reason? The outcome of the war with Paraguay, known as the War of the Triple Alliance.[5]

Paraguay in 1865 was an isolated but expanding economy under the absolute control of the dictator López. Landlocked as it was, in the upper reaches of the Paraná River, the compelling need for a direct outlet to the sea for its exports led to a confrontation with Brazil and Argentina, its far larger and more powerful neighbours (Uruguay was the third and much smaller partner in the alliance). Despite its well-prepared and larger military forces, Paraguay's defeat was devastating. Some 60 per cent of its population (predominantly the men) died in the five years of the conflict! For Brazil and Argentina, the considerable spoils of war were the newly conquered lands, fertile but sparsely populated, of the Gran Chaco, where *yerba mate* – once Paraguay's main export – grew in abundance.

Argentina was already an important agricultural country before the war; together with Brazil, it was the largest economy on the continent. The trade in wheat, dried meat and leather was growing apace, as it had done ever since the country had broken free of its Spanish colonial masters and their monopoly on trade in 1816. Ironically, war had been a highly profitable time for the landowners of the Argentine province of Corrientes, who supplied meat and cereals to all three armies. Argentina's newly acquired 20,000 or so square hectares of land added to its potential wealth, and made it an even more attractive proposition for foreign investors. In fact, between 1860 and 1913, Argentina received 8.5 per cent of the world total of direct foreign investment. And it was Britain that emerged as the largest direct beneficiary of the war, having financed Brazilian armaments, provided war loans to Paraguay and expanded its trade with the Argentines.[6]

THE LAST GAUCHO: THE STORY OF MARTIN FIERRO

'Martin Fierro', the central character of a long epic poem written in two parts (1872 and 1879) by José Hernández,[7] came to represent those generations of skilled horsemen and herders who for centuries occupied the great grasslands south and west of Buenos Aires called the pampas. They were independent and individualistic, their lives a series of nomadic journeys across the pampas, moving their animals in search of pasture, gathering in small communities in settlements rarely containing much more than some makeshift dwellings, a bar and a shop. The work was hard and unforgiving, the culture masculine and brutal. They would gather around camp fires and while they waited for meat to roast, share experiences through the songs and stories passed on from generation to generation, accompanied by the strange seven-string guitar called the *vihuela*. These stories were the myths of a restless population riding the common lands.

> My greatest joy is living free
> Like a bird in the open sky
> I never stop to build a nest
> There's nowhere free of pain
> But no-one here can follow me
> When I take wing and fly.
>
> And I want you all to understand
> When I tell you my sorry tale
> That I'll only fight or kill a man
> When there's nowhere else to go
> And that only the actions of others
> Set me on this wretched path.

Over time there emerged regional chieftains or 'caudillos', with their own bands of horsemen mobilized in the battle for territories of control. Some caudillos became powerful and influential, though they rarely abandoned the characteristic dress and manner of the gaucho: the wide trousers tucked into leather boots, the short poncho and the leather hat.

By the time Martin Fierro came into being, the gaucho way of life, derided by Sarmiento as a brutalizing instinctual existence without morality, violent, arbitrary and short, was in its final moments. The pampas were no longer common lands; they were fenced and divided among the landowners whose animals would later find their way to the slaughterhouses of Buenos Aires and thence make their way to Europe or the United States. As this process of enclosure continued, the gauchos were driven to the margins of the prairie, and often were recruited, as Martin was, to pursue the war of extermination against the Indians who occupied the same marginal areas.

> And they beat you round the body
> And they crack stones on your head
> And never stop to ask how you are
> Or whether you're alive or dead.
> They just throw you in the slammer
> And tie you up in chains.
>
> And that's just the start of your troubles
> The beginning of the end
> There's no way out of this one
> There's just one way out of this door
> To be stuck in a bloody uniform
> And sent to the edge of the world.

The process of civilization drove the Indians from their ancestral lands, while the gauchos, like Martin, who had no love for the Indians, would be charged to pursue them before they themselves were removed from their traditional environment.

Martin, together with his sons, eventually does what many of his contemporaries did. He drifts towards the city, where he lives in the marginal areas on the outskirts to make a living as best he can in the world of petty crime and prostitution. The gaucho becomes, slowly, the 'compadrito', changing his dress but bringing with him the elements of his culture that would contribute to the emergence of the tango.

Martin himself finds this new life intolerable, and returns to the disappearing *pampa* to make a life for himself in a new territory yet to be defined.

> Whether we'll make it or not
> No one on earth can tell
> But we'll ride inland however we can
> Towards the setting sun
> We'll get there sooner or later
> But who knows where or when.

THE CITY BECKONS

The first wave of new arrivals, through the 1860s, would have encouraged their friends and relatives to join them in this promising new Eden. And they responded. From the mid-1860s onwards, immigration increased dramatically as circumstances combined and different interests coincided in making it happen. New investment began to pour into Argentina, principally from Britain but also from the u.s. and France, accelerating the modernization of agriculture and the concentration of land in the hands of a small powerful elite, and expanding the meat trade. The *gauchos* and small farmers expelled from the land settled in shabby townships on the city's outskirts. In Italy, the process of reunification had created new hardships for small farmers, and nearly 100,000 Italian migrants took ship across the Atlantic to Argentina through the 1870s. Expelled from their small farms, and threatened by the latest cholera epidemic, they came from the rural areas of Piedmont, Liguria and Lombardy via Genoa and Naples. Artisans and tradesmen marginalized by industrialization joined them on the migrant ships, encouraged by the promise of an open border, accommodation on arrival, and a train ticket to the interior of the country where they would be able to find a piece of land to farm. The railways built by foreign capitalists in the previous decade were opening up the interior of Argentina. Anyone in good health and under sixty would be accepted.

Young men came from Spain, particularly from regions like Galicia, where rural poverty and the threat of obligatory military service accelerated their decision. Others came also from central Europe, from Poland and Russia, driven by hunger and persecution; the majority of these groups of migrants were Jews.

The young immigrants often left their families behind in the home country, where the women and the elderly scratched a living on tiny plots. It was a pattern across Europe. The men would surely have left amid tears and regrets, reassuring those left behind that

Freshly arrived immigrants at the docks, Buenos Aires.

they would make their fortunes soon and call for their wives and families once as they were settled. And they would have meant every word.

Not all the migrants were men, however. Abandoned and impoverished women have always found the route of prostitution open to them. And the promise of Argentina appealed to them too.

Paradoxically, Orthodox Jewish women left by their husbands or widowed had very few alternative options; they were forbidden from finding new partners and restricted in the work they could do. The networks of Eastern European Jewish procurers exploited the situation to their advantage. Over 60 per cent of registered prostitutes in Argentina at the end of the decade were foreign born, with Polish, Russian or Austro-Hungarian citizens among them.[8] Perhaps they imagined that the booming Argentine economy would offer them other opportunities, but women's employment there remained very limited – mainly domestic service or shop work – at very low wages.

In Britain, in particular, the myth of the white slave traffic filled the scandal sheets and the penny dreadfuls. The reformers and morality campaigners rose in high dudgeon in their turn and retailed stories of respectable young English women kidnapped at night and deposited by force in the bordellos of Buenos Aires. In reality, the British consul could find almost no cases to confirm the legend – but the rumours persisted nonetheless. In fact, it was Eastern European women who would have been most likely to have been entrapped by organizations of pimps. Those who travelled to the riverside red-light districts from Western Europe were impelled by poverty rather than sinister criminal bands roaming the night streets of Paris or London.

It was the expanding market for their sexual services, among this population of men far from home, that explained the dramatic expansion of the sex industry in this same period. There were, of course, equally large numbers of local women working the streets or in dubious music halls and cafés as waitresses; they too had come from the interior of the country in search of the riches that the myth of Buenos Aires promised them.

For all of them, Paradise proved less easily accessible than they had imagined. Some immigrants accepted their free rail tickets to the interior; the majority, however, did not, and those who did go in search of a plot of land for a small farm were for the most part disappointed. The big landowners resisted any attempts to diversify land ownership. When they did offer small, largely infertile plots for rent or sharecropping, they would arbitrarily take them back to prevent any claims to permanence. In the event, many immigrants soon returned to the cities, while most remained in Buenos Aires, or in cities like Santa Fe. Buenos Aires was the federal capital, the heartland of the economy, and a thriving port where work could always be found.

From 1870 onwards, the city lived through a dramatic period of growth, as the wealthy classes whose income derived from the land built a city that expressed both their growing prosperity and their cultural and social aspirations to be a second Paris at the other end of the world. As it grew, its wide avenues, like Avenida 5 de Mayo, its European stores and shopfronts, its elegant restaurants, theatres, and café-concerts mimicked the city where all bourgeois Argentines imagined themselves living someday. As is so often the case, it was immigrant labourers who built the new city, though at night they returned to a very different world around its edges.

In the city, the new arrivals came face to face with others who had also recently arrived in the slums around the port. There were the rural populations who had lost their living space and who had drifted towards the burgeoning city. There were others who came from Brazil and Uruguay, some left behind as the flotsam of the recently completed war, others freed from slavery in Brazil a few years earlier and moving south in search of work.

The immigrants met, or clashed, in the unlit streets close to the river. They shared neither a language nor a history at first, yet eventually in these crowded alleys they, their cultures, their languages, and their rhythms would merge as they learned to dance – and survive – together.

LIVES AT THE MARGINS

The living spaces of the poor, native and foreign born, were very different from the grand houses and mansions of the city centre and the middle-class suburbs. In 1871, an epidemic of yellow fever in the south of the city, where most of the richer families then lived, drove them to look for new homes in healthier environments. They moved north, to the areas that still remain the habitat of the prosperous – Florida, Belgrano and the Barrio Norte. The grand houses they left behind, their patios and backyards, and the alleys in between, became home to hundreds of families moving towards the capital, where they lived in makeshift rooms, each housing at least one family, surrounding open courtyards with shared sinks. These were the *conventillos*, where the immigrants mingled with the refugees from the countryside in an overcrowded and promiscuous environment.

> The sediment of the population flowed across the wet floor; the rooms were small and narrow, and through their open doors you could glimpse the grubby rooms, full of boxes and trunks, broken chairs and tables with three legs, mouldy mirrors, comic strips pinned to the walls, and that strange disorder wherever four or six sleep together, and where everything has to be given a place somewhere.

> Outside the door a metal pan is boiling . . . and the floor is covered with potato peelings, onion skins, cabbage leaves. They mark the room's frontier, just as the fences mark the limits of the great pampa ranches . . . [9]

The majority of European immigrants crowded into these *conventillos*, or into the ramshackle wooden houses on the riverbank in the areas close to the docks. La Boca, with its brightly painted facades, housed them in suffocating intimacy. Most of the new arrivals were men between fifteen and thirty years old, far from home and marginalized from the host culture (despite the formal welcome that had been extended to them), without their families, and yearning for affection and the comfort of women. This concentration of young males created a world of repressed sexual desire, well served by the burgeoning sex

industry, in an atmosphere of male competition and ritual
violence.

In these early days the immigrants would huddle together in
the face of a cold and unwelcoming city. The Italians gathered in
La Boca district whose painted houses reminded them of Genoa
or Naples. The Spaniards, who were the second largest group,
gathered on the Avenida de Mayo, while the Jews of Eastern
Europe hovered around the Plaza 11 de Septiembre. The English
migrants were for the most part entrepreneurs and chose to live
beside their Argentine associates in and around Belgrano. And in
the suburbs, the *arrabales*, the recent arrivals from the *pampa* played
their guitars and remembered the homes they had left behind.

In every area the language and habits of home were repeated
and reproduced. And while the different groups met regularly in the
crowded streets down by the river, their relationship was tense and
suspicious in this first decade of the new Argentina. The young men
roamed the streets, watching and listening, waiting for the moment
when they could visit the brothels whose tantalizing music filled
the night streets. The working week was long and tough. Going
home in the evening through dark streets must at times have been

A typical
conventillo.

25

frightening. Home was a *conventillo* – noisy, crowded and dirty. You might share one room, where you lodged with a family. And each week the tension would rise as the time for the landlord's weekly visit approached. He might throw some families out, raise the rents arbitrarily, or drive more families into the overcrowded space. Small wonder that the street seemed so seductive.

In the 1870s, the beautification of Buenos Aires had hardly begun; the streets in the poor districts were not lit, and the conditions that had given rise to the yellow fever epidemic remained. But there was one day of rest. And there would always be a good set of clothes for Saturday night – a clean white shirt, freshly laundered by some young mother, shoes cracked but shiny, trousers narrow at the ankle. Brothels were legalized in the poorer areas of Buenos Aires by 1875, but the rules were strict – they could not be within two blocks of a church or a school and the women could not be seen on the street or at the windows. But you could still hear the music from the street.

The existence of these brothels was a paradox. Four years before their legalization a Civil Code was published which defined the proper role of women as that of marriage and procreation. The decision to seek work, any kind of work, placed them in the category of fallen women, whose existence outside the home consigned them to the demi-monde of the street, just one step away from prostitution. Against that background the existence of legal bordellos seems less liberal than might at first appear to be the case. It could be seen rather as a policy of containment in an era obsessed with the risks of venereal disease as well as yellow fever.[10] While the new immigrant labourers were indispensable for economic growth, it was imperative that they were kept away from the glistening new middle-class areas.

Other women plied their trade outside the law; they were the waitresses in the cafés or the local music halls. They would take you to their room in a cheap lodging house, or stand against you in a dark alley. But in the brothels there were exotic women – French prostitutes with beautiful names, like the Madame Ivonne of Cadícamo's tango – to drink and dance with for a minute or two before the brief sexual encounter in an upstairs room.

On a busy night there would be a long wait in the edgy queues that surrounded the buildings in the darkness. There would be occasional fights over people who tried to jump the queue; sometimes the pimps, the *cafishios*, would emerge from the shadows to offer some quicker satisfactions in the local cafés or recommend their charges who were working inside; they might even offer a demonstration of their charges' prowess in a dance of sometimes obscene suggestiveness to the music issuing from within.

Only prostitutes danced in the Buenos Aires of the late nineteenth century, and they were not allowed into the street. So the men practised as they waited by dancing on the cobbles.

This was the birthplace of tango, and these were the actors in the tango drama. It is a story of encounters in a public space that is lawless, in construction, unsafe and full of marauding men and women hovering in expectation of an opportunity to cheat, to steal, or most importantly, to seduce. For in the end, the prelude to everything else is the seduction. In this male-dominated world, the tango dramatized the struggles between men for possession of women, and (from the predominantly male point of view) the cynical way in which the women exploited the loneliness and frustration of men.

TANGO: A DANCE IS BORN

There is endless debate and dispute over the origins of tango; inevitably so for a dance born in the shadows. Its provocative movements and bizarre combination of sexuality and distance would seem to confirm the contention of those like the writer Jorge Luis Borges, who insisted that it was a dance exclusive to the brothel. It was surely born in the street, in the cafés and brothels of the port city. But it is more, much more, than a sexual entertainment.

The dance itself is a marriage – a 'three-minute marriage', as some have suggested – an encounter between traditions far wider than the pimp's propaganda. The twisting of the body – the *firuletes* and *cortes* – must surely have its origins in the dances of the black communities, the *tangos de negros* banned by the Municipal Court of Montevideo in the 1850s as lewd and obscene.[11] It might also have found those same movements in the tango of Andalusia. The elegant and complex footwork could have come from the fast *tarantella* of Northern Italy. But the embrace belonged to the *habaneras* that brought the European contredanse to Latin America via Cuba, brought perhaps by sailors who gave it its other name, the *marinera*. And the native addition to the mix was the *milonga*, the country dance that accompanied the rural exiles of the *arrabales* and the *compadritos* who claimed it for their own in the city.

> The tango was simultaneously a ritual and a spectacle of traumatic encounters between people who should never have come together.[12]

These dramas of challenge and transgression had their own very particular cast of characters. The theatre was the street – the ill-lit, unpaved streets of the dockland districts, or the lanes around the slaughterhouses, where the cattlemen came and went in their squeaking carts. The dance, at this first moment of its birth, was a wary meeting, its signs mute at first, though it would soon develop a language of its own, both a language of gesture and a new speech – *lunfardo* – which was itself a meeting, a fusion of languages and codes that were both inclusive (of this new riverside population) and exclusive (of the other Buenos Aires growing up in the centre and the north of the city). *Lunfardo* was a secret language shared by a new community whose members were linked only by their marginality and their vulnerability. It is hard at this distance to know to what extent it was a spoken language, an authentic argot spoken to conceal and challenge the Spanish (or French or English) of bourgeois city folk. What we know of it is its second life, as the expression of an authentic experience viewed retrospectively, nostalgically, by the first generation to create a poetry in *lunfardo* that aspired to speak to an audience beyond the world of the docks.

In its early manifestations, *lunfardo* was a functional code that made possible the first interactions between immigrant communities that remained to a considerable extent isolated and enclosed to themselves. It arose and was forged at first in the spaces of social interchange and shared experience. It was also the language of the street, the brothel and the criminal underclass. A basic *lunfardo* vocabulary list provides several alternative words for prostitutes, pimps and brothels; it offers several variants for confidence tricksters and silver-tongued persuaders; it provides a number of ways to describe knives and the scars they leave on the face (*feite, barbijo*). The fraternity of thieves is divided by its particular skills; the *culatero*, for example, specializes in stealing from the back pockets of his targets. And this assortment of spivs, con men and flyboys has names for all its victims from the wealthy *bacán* who pays well for his mistress (his *mina*) whom he keeps in a *bulín*, to the soft fool and easy touch *boludo* or *gil*. And in permanent attendance are the corrupt police, moneylenders and fences who oversee this network of mutual small-scale exploitation.

When men danced together, they would mimic the pimp's promises or reenact an actual or imagined knife fight with the country boys who strolled the streets as if they owned them – and took very little persuasion to demonstrate their skill with the short knife – the *facón* – that was part of the uniform of the *gaucho*. Like the *malevo* (the criminal), the pimp restrains himself until the prettiest girl in the dance hall provokes him to fight.

Se cruzó
un gran rencor y otro rencor
a la luz
de un farolito a querosén
y un puñal
que parte en dos un corazón
porque así
lo quiso aquella cruel mujer.

Cuentan los que vieron
que los guapos
culebrearon
con su cuerpos
y buscaron
afanosos
el descuido
del contrario
y en un claro
de la guardia
hundió el mozo
de Palermo
hasta el mango
su facón.

Anger met with anger / *in the light of a paraffin lamp* /
and a knife that / *would cut a heart in two* / *flashed because*
a cruel woman / *had wanted it so.* / *Those who were there said* /
the two men / *swerved and swayed their bodies* / *while they*
watched / *alert* / *for the other to make a false move* / *or to lower*
his guard / *when the kid from Palermo* / *buried his knife in the*
other / *to the hilt.*

   ('La puñalada', The Slashing – Celedonio Flores, 1937)

The fight, the two men swerving and moving their bodies around one another in anticipation of a strike, seems more dance than battle, and the precursor to an encounter that would later be endlessly relived, albeit without a blade, as tango.

In those early years the whole complex life of the community found expression in the physical theatre of dance. There would certainly have been singers improvising verses to the playing of the bands. Since they played in brothels and cafés, their content would surely have been mostly erotic, explicitly or obliquely, like the blues verses that have come to us from the riverside brothels of the South of the United States. In this phase of transition too, the rural tradition of Argentina itself, the *payador* or travelling troubadour who improvised couplets at local festivals and other social gatherings to the accompaniment of the seven-stringed guitar which was the predecessor of the contemporary instrument, was very much alive in Buenos Aires. The growing city had drawn in people from the countryside but in its expansion it had also absorbed rural communities around its edges. The newly emerging tango incorporated the rhythms of traditional music too, most significantly and enduringly the traditional *milonga,* whose fast pace defined the first tangos.

The early dancers still wore the *gaucho'*s wide trousers and high boots and the short poncho and flat wide-brimmed hat that commemorated the days of horses and open common spaces of the pre-modern *pampa*. But that would give way very soon to a different uniform, to a dress that reflected not the origins of the immigrant population but its newly constructed reality. This contradictory, fragile, often dangerous world was represented by the *compadrito*.

ENTER THE COMPADRITO

He may have arrived carrying a guitar, wearing the clothes of the *gaucho*, but he had left his horse behind. What he had brought

Compadritos.

with him from his settlement on the *pampas* was his memory, and the traditional songs and the rhythms of their country dances – the *chacarera* and the *milonga*. In the poor districts around the city or among the abandoned mansions of the centre he would have found lodging of some kind. But he was still the *compadre* – the man of the country.

The city did not allow him the luxury of remaining that way for very long. Survival in the city demanded new skills and new attitudes that would serve him best in the bruising encounters with the young men and women who had come from Europe to share this new urban space. He came from a world where survival was equally precarious, which is why his songs so often celebrated his prowess with horse and lariat, his skill as a fighter, and his successes as a lover. The myths, at least, were adaptable to the new environment, where he was equally required to show flexibility, skill, and the wisdom of the street. More often than not he proved ill-adapted to work, and instead he cruised the muddy streets, observing his *china* (his girl), or seeking out a chance to steal or cheat or misdirect some innocent passing stranger.

Now he was the *compadrito*, the *compadre 'venido a menos'* (come down in the world):

> Instead of becoming only an urban Don Juan, the compadrito became a pimp. As skillful and valiant a fighter as the compadre, he became, not a defender of rights, but a bully, a robber, and at times a killer.[13]

Most were less than killers, but many were pimps and confidence tricksters. And as their prestige grew, so they abandoned the short ponchos and glistening black boots in favour of the tight- fitting suits, high heels, spats and long, brilliantined hair depicted on so many posters and paintings (and in so many tangos) of the day. And with time, he might repeat, albeit in very different circumstances, his grandfather's role as the servant of a local chieftain or *caudillo*, although one that had exchanged spurs and saddle for the frock coat of the parliamentarian.

> The compadrito was the man of the tango. And the tango was his dance, its choreographic style based on his affectations, developed in the brothels he ran on the edges of Buenos Aires.[14]

He no longer danced in the country style, whirling and jumping as his partner mirrored him and held high her whirling skirts. He had taken on the style of the bourgeois – or at least his own version of it – mimicked his dress and assumed his seductive posture, his obvious superiority in comparison to the girls he came to find in his descent into the *arrabal*. The *compadrito* would rarely have ventured beyond the edges of the barrio, but he would have increasingly seen the arrogant young men of Belgrano and the Barrio Norte come down to his world. And in the dance he posed and proffered this newly learned self, and also remembered the swift evasions and feints that had served him well in the drunken knife duels on the *pampa*. Outside the brothels, he may well have moved along the queue of men outside, moving his body to the music in suggestive anticipation of what was to come. From time to time he would draw out another man to practise his imminent moves or, in the better establishments, to anticipate the brief dance the client might expect in the hall before moving up to the bedroom.

This then was a new music, born in a modern city divided into immigrant ghettoes and the wealthier quarters where the middle classes lived. Directly and indirectly, the tango both echoed that gulf that separated the city from itself and provided its poetic voice. When it found its voice, it was that of a man who sang about women as lovers, as instruments and as sacrificing mothers. It also spoke of ambition and of the battle for survival that drained the tango and its music of any sentimentality. For this was a deep song of rootless people fighting the city and one another in order to survive, and both celebrating and resenting the marginality to which they were condemned by those who benefited from their labour.

The barrio, the *conventillo*, the *arrabal* were transformed as the tango developed in a way that idealized both the evils of the place and its deficiencies – the absence of solidarity, the fleeting pleasures of a life hard lived.

> *Eran otros hombres más hombres los nuestros.*
> *No se conocían cocó ni morfina,*
> *los muchachos de antes no usaban gomina*
> *¿Te acordás hermano? ¡Qué tiempos aquéllos!*
> *Veinticinco abriles que no volverán*

Veinticinco abriles, volver a tenerlos
Si cuando me acuerdo me pongo a llorar
¿Dónde están los muchachos de entonces?
Barra antigua de ayer, ¿dónde está?
Yo y vos solos quedamos hermano,
Yo y vos solos para recordar . . .
¿Dónde están las mujeres aquéllas
minas fieles, de gran corazón
que en los bailes de Laura peleaban
cada cual defendiendo su amor?

Men were more men in those days / they never used cocaine or morphine / the lads then used no grease on their hair. / Remember brother? What times they were! / Twenty-five Aprils that will never return now / Twenty-five Aprils, I wish I could have them again / When I remember I start to weep. / Where are the lads of those days? / Where's the old bar we used to go to? / There's just you and me left, brother / just the two of us to remember . . . / Where are the women, those women / loyal and generous / who would get into fights at Laura's dance hall / each defending her own lover?
('Tiempos Viejos', Old Time – Manuel Romero, 1926)

For the moment, the other Buenos Aires was closed to them, emphasizing their exclusion, their loneliness, their invisibility. But Buenos Aires was changing its shape and its appearance, building a new metropolis with the labour of the tango-dancing immigrants. Eventually the walls between would begin to fracture and a traffic would begin between the halves of the divided city. And when it did, tango would play its central part.

2 A CITY DIVIDED

THE BIRTH OF A METROPOLIS

By 1880, Buenos Aires was ready for its new clothes and its new face. The village by the river had grown and spread. It had split into two worlds whose occasional contact was enough to create aspirations among the new immigrants in the slums and fantasies of desire among the middle classes gazing across at the transgressive and forbidden worlds down by the docks.

Argentina had changed profoundly in the previous decade. Roca's last war against the Indian populations in 1879 had not only driven them to the margins – it had also, more profoundly, made the indigenous peoples invisible to the new urban culture. The *pampas* were now enclosed as large working farms serving the burgeoning export trade. The *gauchos* who had spent their lives riding the wide grasslands were gone now – not disappeared, but transformed into shiftless wanderers in the darkened streets of the poor suburbs, the *arrabales*. In 1880, Buenos Aires was formally named the federal capital of the republic. The battle that had marked the years since formal independence in 1816 between the capital, with its European connection, and the interior provinces, whose horizons were in Latin America, was now finally resolved in the city's favour. The implications were profound. It was not just a question of where the administration of the country was located. It was a decision about how it would develop economically, and what expressions of nationhood would prevail. It was a decision about how Argentines would see themselves, and what kind of

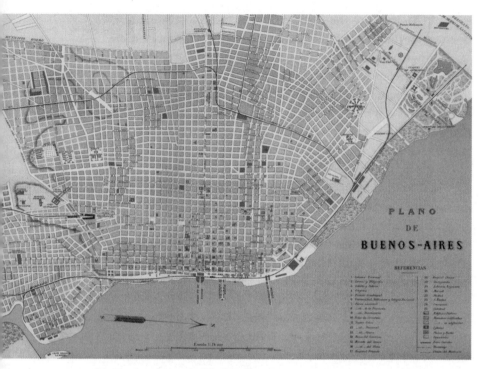

PLANO
DE
BUENOS-AIRES

REFERENCIAS

Nineteenth-century map of Buenos Aires.

society would emerge from the fusions and encounters that were shaping the new capital.

The material changes were dramatic. Between 1872 and 1888 the amount of land under cultivation had risen from 600,000 hectares (about 1,500,000 acres) to 2.5 million as Argentina fast became a major producer of cereals for export. Just 20 years before, it had been importing wheat and flour! The number of sheep increased sixfold in the same period, as exports of meat and wool grew at an extraordinary rate. And in the province of Buenos Aires, surrounding the capital, some five million cattle grazed; later their numbers would also increase at speed.[1] With Buenos Aires as its capital, the Argentine economy was now confirmed as export-led – its wool and meat and hides and cereals were all destined for Europe, and all passed through the growing port city.

The agricultural products were transported to the docks across the fast expanding rail network, mostly financed by British investors. In 1857, the country boasted just six miles of track; by 1890 that had extended to 5,800 miles. It is unlikely, of course, that any of these changes (and they were dramatic in their speed and breadth) would have been possible without the immigrant populations.[2]

In the far south, the Welsh colonists enticed to Patagonia in the mid-1860s were important sheep farmers.[3] In Mendoza it was (unsurprisingly) French and Italian immigrants who drove wine production forward. But if many of them had come hoping for a piece of land to cultivate, they were mostly disappointed. They rarely managed to fulfil that dream. The bulk of immigrants made their way back to the cities, and principally to Buenos Aires, where they could find work on the docks or in construction, or in the small factories now being set up (often by wealthier immigrants) producing textiles, cigarettes and food products. Later, many would work in the slaughterhouses and meat packing plants that became increasingly central to the economy.

This newly modernizing Argentina remained a country dominated by large landowners. And they were growing very rich very quickly, not just from the goods and products they exported, but also from the lucrative land deals always associated with the laying of the railways, not to mention the earnings of lawyers and others in attendance! (Think how many Hollywood Westerns have the battle between farmers and the railway companies as a central theme.)

But the small layer of people who were growing rich in this boom period would not, by and large, be found ensconced in their rural mansions. The management of their lands would be left to stewards and foremen, while the propertied classes took themselves to the capital to enjoy the benefits brought to them by others. The capital's new status demanded a transformation that would leave no one arriving in the city in any doubt that they were entering what would very soon be the largest city in South America – and the heart of an unprecedented economic boom.

As always, the symbolic home of civilization was Paris; a Mecca towards which every middle-class and bourgeois Argentine looked. And Paris too was in the throes of a magnificent transformation that continued the work begun under the direction of Baron Haussmann. His ideal in city planning was 'long straight streets' and wide avenues, where 'the temples of the bourgeoisie's spiritual and secular power' would find expression.[4] Walter Benjamin describes the Baron's 'love of demolition' that expropriated and swept away the old town, though his impulse came from a political need: to ensure that the barricades that had blocked the narrow streets during the short-lived workers' government of the Commune in 1871 would never appear again. Nevertheless, all the Argentine visitor saw were the Champs Élysées, as wide as a river, and the grand palaces and mansions around the Place de la Concorde. *That* was a proud, modern city.

Immigrants on the gangplank.

The mayor (or *Intendente*) of Buenos Aires between 1880 and 1887 was Torcuato de Alvear, and he oversaw the emergence of the new city out of the ashes of the old. The Avenida 5 de Mayo was turned into the vast avenue it is today (though it would later be surpassed by the even wider Avenida 9 de Julio). He expanded the city's main square, the Plaza de Mayo, thousands of trees were planted and parks laid out by the French director of city parks, Carlos Thays. New public buildings and private mansions announced their civic pride. The grand new stations imitated their European counterparts, and paid homage to the critical importance of the railways. And trams, horse-drawn at first but electrified by 1900, carried the growing population from place to place.

This prosperous and optimistic urban middle class demanded its own street life, though one very different from the unlit alleys of La Boca and Nueva Pompeya. They had elegant streetlights and well-lit cafés and restaurants, as well as cabarets and theatres. From there you could not see the dimly lit slums down by the riverbank; they remained physically and socially invisible, though the middle classes were increasingly uneasy about the proximity of this population of the lower depths.

MEANWHILE . . .

While the law of 1875 had made brothels legal subject to stringent conditions, the Civil Code, published in 1871, had stressed the importance of the family, and the role of women as exemplary mothers. The paradox, or perhaps we should call it 'hypocrisy', persisted; the Code's condition of existence was the marginalization of that other obscure world of the poor. The obsession with 'infection', the endless public debates over venereal disease, the fascination with the forbidden, all testify to the contradiction. And for a decade or two, the two worlds were successfully kept apart.

The poor areas of the city supplied a working class for the new factories, most of them small plants at first, and for the larger factories that would spread through the Barracas district, later (and still) called Avellaneda. As the city was beautified and transformed, the prostitutes – or at least the majority of the street and café workers – were expelled from the upper-class districts. The elegant brothels catering to the upper middle class, like La Casa de Laura, however, were never closed. And there were growing numbers of women seeking work in the brothels. The transformation of the countryside, and the shortage of rural employment, brought a new generation of women to the shadowy demi-monde of cafés and *academias*.

Yo soy la Morocha
La más agraciada,
La más renombrada
De esta población.
Soy la que al paisano
Muy de madrugada
Brinda un cimarrón . . .

Soy la morocha argentina,
La que no siente pesares,
Y alegre pasa la vida
Con sus cantares.

Soy la gentil compañera
Del noble gaucho porteño
La que conserva la vida
Para su dueño.

I am the Brown Girl / the best endowed / the most famous woman / in this town / I'm the one the countryman / early in the morning / makes a present of a pony to . . .

I'm the Argentine brown girl / who feels no sorrow / and cheerfully spends her life / singing her songs.
I'm the charming companion / to the noble gaucho of these plains / the woman who protects the life / of her master.

('La Morocha', The Brown Girl – Ángel Villoldo, 1905)

The majority of *registered* prostitutes were foreign women, for whom registration offered some minimal degree of protection, even if it involved paying off the police on a regular basis. And the disproportion of men to women (170 men per 100 women) guaranteed a growing clientele, as immigration picked up again through the 1880s after a brief lull at the end of the previous decade.

The 1880s and 1890s brought other opportunities for employment for women outside the home, as they found work in the factories producing food or clothing, or sewing the sacks for the growing quantities of cereals that the country exported. The bulk of those who worked, however, still found positions in domestic service. In the 1890s, some would find work in the elegant department stores opening their doors on the Calle Florida – the most famous of which, Harrod's, was opened later, in 1914. By 1895, 20 per cent of the workforce were women. Some of them, of course, would have supplemented their wage labour with extra hours as waitresses downtown.

The men, waiting in the queues outside the brothels for their opportunity to dance, might have found the street a freer place to be than the overcrowded slums they returned to after a day's work on the construction of the new city.

Tango remained the dance of the lower depths; the expression of the strange merger of people and communities that was the melting pot where the new Argentina was being formed. Since the women were relatively few, and their time for dancing restricted, the men would practise in the street or in the *academias*. The musicians who played for them were workers like themselves

An early twentieth-
century tango
quartet.

who often played through the night before leaving for work early
the next morning. Their trios, most commonly comprising the
flute, violin and harp (the guitar, the clarinet and the emblematic
bandoneon came later), played the fast, improvised rhythms of the
new dance, associated in style and location with the underworld of
pimps and prostitutes. It was still marked by its origins in the black
population, from whom came the elaborate twisting and jerking
of the body which so appalled the respectable ladies of the city.

And the fast, tripping pace owed much to the rural *milonga*. It
is significant that a very high proportion of tango musicians at this
early stage were African Argentine. Their music made no bones
about its function as an advertisement for the coitus to follow;

and the improvised lyrics, of which we have only a fragmentary knowledge, fulfilled the same function. Like the early blues songs, they were largely improvised around erotic suggestion or plain bawdiness. While it is not clear when lyrics began to be written down, 'Dame la lata' (1884) has a claim to be the first written tango. *La lata* was the metal token with which clients paid their dancers; the speaker/singer here is obviously the *compadrito* or *cafishio*, that is, the pimp.

> *Qué vida mas arrastrada*
> *la del pobre canfinflero,*
> *el lunes cobra las latas,*
> *el martes anda fulero.*
>
> *Dame la lata que has escondido,*
> *¿Qué te pensás, bagayo,*
> *que yo soy filo?*
> *Dame la lata y ¡a laburar!*
> *Si no la linda biaba*
> *te vas a ligar.*

> *The pimp's life / is a rotten life, / Monday he cashes the tokens in / By Tuesday flat broke again.*
> *Give me the tokens you've hidden away / Who d'you think you are, you ugly cow, / Think I'm a fool? / Give me the chips and get to work / If you don't all you'll get / Is the back of my hand.*
> *('Dame la Lata', Give me the token – Anon., 1884)*

The manner of the dance was changing as the 1880s wore on. The barrio was evolving its special secret languages of exclusion, the street slang and underworld argot, like *Cocoliche* and *lunfardo*. As the idiom developed, the first lyricists began slowly to move beyond the bawdy calls and write brief verses to punctuate the music. And the musicians too found more work for themselves as the bordellos, cafés and *academias* proliferated.

Tango was becoming permanent, just as the immigrant population began to reshape its relationship to the city in these last two decades of the century. Their sense of impermanence and marginality, their fragile hold on the city, reflected their world of work, of casual, badly paid labour and the absence of any forms of collective organization. Indeed, wages fell significantly between 1875 and 1879 in the city, and in agriculture, particularly in the distant sugar-producing areas around Tucumán, the already poor wages fell by 30 per cent – when they were paid at all. For in many rural areas, the truck system or forms of sharecropping persisted even as Buenos Aires was trying on its Parisian outfits. By the 1880s, the rise of industries associated with the export boom, together with stable employment for men and women in factories and shops, slowly and at first imperceptibly transformed the shifting populations of the *arrabales* and the *conventillos*. They were becoming workers, albeit highly exploited ones – and their relationship with the city and society was changing. By the end of the decade, tango too was becoming established.

FORBIDDEN PLACES

> Those people turned their back on us, the immigrants. We were the unclean masses . . . The rich people crowded together in their exclusive areas and grumbled about their resentment at the invasion of the mob, the wretches who survived however they could, begging, stealing, whoring . . .

> Because the striking workers were always Germans or Poles or Italians or French or Spaniards or Jews. Very few of them were Argentine. That was how the rich spoke about the nation and the racist ideas they liked to bandy about.[5]

For the urban middle classes, the docks and the dark streets of the barrio were always the source of a deep ambiguity. On the one hand, they were seduced and excited by the shadowy figures from this other world, and the image of a world of luxurious bordellos, of beautiful women dancing naked, of forbidden music hidden behind velvet curtains. On the other hand, they were repelled by that universe of temptation and sexuality on the very edge of Sodom and Gomorrah. Intellectuals like Leopoldo Lugones and Manuel Gálvez thundered against the immorality that undermined the decent order predicated in the 1871 Civil Code. The very presence of these places threatened family life and the good Christian order anticipated in the Code. Emile Zola's brutally naturalist novels, with their underlying theory of genetic sinfulness, found imitators in the Argentina of the late nineteenth century, where the weak sinner and the devious woman of the streets would have their first outing.[6]

The fear of disease, of the syphilis and gonorrhoea they imagined to be lurking in this shadowy and corrupt environment, exercised both the feminists and the Christian ladies in equal measure. And the growing numbers of women workers came to be seen as a kind of bridge between these two worlds.

Although they had chosen the route of honest labour to maintain themselves and their dependents, the working women had nevertheless opted for a world outside the family and for a degree of independence; that gave them a freedom which could – and would, the conservatives argued – lead them inexorably into the circle of corruption and sin that beckoned to them from the dockside. The very fact that they worked was enough for them to be considered loose women who neglected their children, even though Argentine law permitted women to work and trade at eighteen, albeit not to marry until they were 21. Yet these working women appear very rarely in the lyrics of tango; they existed in a no man's land.

So the attitudes of both sides of this divided city could be expressed and interpreted through their attitude to the tango. The middle class shuddered with revulsion at the overt sexuality of the dance which was also beginning to find expression in lyrics that must have found their way into their areas; lyrics that were crude and brutal in their description of the sexual relations between men and women, and which, furthermore, spoke in the bizarre language of this other, threatening world.

In the poor districts of the growing city, tango remained – for the same reasons – inextricably interwoven with the underworld of pimps and prostitutes, hucksters and tricksters, pickpockets and thieves. But it was a world familiar to their populations, and above all to the men who frequented their local bordello as much to escape momentarily from the promiscuity of the overcrowded *conventillos* and *arrabales* as for the music and the sex. Yet the barrio was changing. The immigrant population was settling into permanence, and many of the casual labourers of the early years were becoming waged workers as industry, and the city, expanded.

The tango, too, was becoming resident in the city, and was now the sound of a stable community. Tango lyrics began to be written down and the first generation of lyricists emerged in the new world by the river, where the expanding docks also provided more work for the continuing flow of immigrants. Their lives were beginning to find some reflection in the words written by this first generation of tango poets. Silverio Manco wrote his crudely suggestive songs in the most impenetrable *lunfardo*; Alfredo Eusebio Gobbi, the father of one of the most famous musicians of tango's future Golden Age, was another lyricist and singer. Ángel Villoldo (1861–1919) was probably the best known and among the most prolific writers of tangos in the first decade of the century; he was also a key figure in this moment of transition and change. For the barrios, the poor working-class districts, were beginning to find their voice through tango – and tango was pressing at the barriers that divided the city.

Villoldo recorded many of the dramatis personae of this unfolding drama. He was a recognizable figure in the underworld of Buenos Aires. A singer, a dancer, a musician (he played guitar and harmonica, at the same time), he drew the threads of tango together around him. 'La Morocha' was one of his most famous and iconic lyrics; he wrote the music for another, equally emblematic piece – 'El Choclo' – to which words were later added by Enrique Santos Discépolo. But his 1903 tango called 'El Porteñito' laid out the scenario for generations of tangos to come.

Soy hijo de Buenos Aires
por apodo 'El Porteñito'
el criollo más compadrito
que en esta tierra nació.
Cuando un tango en la viguela
rasguea algún compañero
no hay nadie en el mundo entero
que baile mejor que yo.
No hay ninguno que me iguale
para enamorar mujeres
. . . Soy el terror del malevaje
cuando en un baile me meto,
porque a ninguno respeto
de los que hay en la reunión.
Y si alguno se retoba
y viene haciéndose el guapo
la mando de un castañazo
a buscar quien lo engrupió.

I'm a son of Buenos Aires / they call me 'El Porteñito' / the smartest compadrito / born in this country. / When some comrade

/ strums a tango on his guitar (vihuela) / there's no one in the world / dances better than me. / No one gets the better of me / when it comes to seducing women / . . . I'm the terror of the bad lads / when I go dancing / because I respect no one / there at the party. / And if someone gets smart / and tries putting on airs / I'll deal him a smack in the face / and send him to look for some other smart aleck.

('El porteñito', The City Kid – Ángel Villoldo, 1903)

Villoldo was also a worker, at different times a printworker and a carter, carrying loads to and from the port, so he was also a participant in the unfolding story of working-class organization and resistance. The early trade unions were being formed as the nineteenth century drew to its end, influenced above all by the anarchist ideas, which Villoldo himself shared, carried across the ocean from Spain and Italy.

Es el siglo en que vivimos
de lo más original
el progreso nos ha dado una vida artificial.
Muchos caminan a máquina
porque es viejo andar a pie,
hay extractos de alimentos
y hay quien pasa sin comer.
Siempre hablamos de progreso
buscando la perfección
y reina el arte moderno
en todita su extensión.
La chanchulla y la matufia
hoy forman la sociedad
y nuestra vida moderna
es una calamidad.

De unas drogas hacen vino
y de porotos café,
de maní es el chocolate
y de yerbas es el té.
. . . La leche se 'pastoriza'
con el agua y almidón
y con carne de ratones
se fabrica el salchichón.
Hoy la matufia está en boga
y siempre crecerá más
y mientras el pobre trabaja
y no hace más que pagar.
Señores, abrir el ojo
y no acostarse a dormir,
hay que estudiar con provecho
el gran arte de vivir.

In this century of ours / this very original time / progress has given
us an artificial life. / Lots of people travel in cars / because walking
is old hat / there is food everywhere / and there are people with
nothing to eat. / We talk about progress / looking for perfection /
and the modern arts prevail / everywhere you look. / trickery and
cheating / are what society's about today / and our modern life /
is a calamity.
The wine's made of drugs / and the coffee of kidney beans / the
chocolate's made with peanuts / and the tea is really grass . . . /
Milk is 'pastorized' / with water and starch / and sausages are
made / from the flesh of mice. / Trickery's in fashion / and more so
every day / and the poor man keeps on working / and keeps on paying
out. / Ladies and gentlemen, open your eyes / and don't just go to
sleep / it's time to study carefully / the great art of living.

> *('Matufias o el arte de vivir', Trickery or the art of living*
> *– Ángel Villoldo, 1904?)*

TANGO COMES OUT OF THE SHADOWS

Villoldo deserved his reputation as the troubadour of the changing immigrant community. But he was also part of the first generation of tango artists whose renown spread beyond La Boca and Nueva Pompeya as the city expanded. The prelude to tango's emergence from the darkened streets down by the docks was musical, a moment both symbolized and in some sense made possible by the arrival from Germany at the end of the 1880s of a new instrument: the powerful, large accordion first developed as a substitute for the harmonium in religious services. And the bandoneon has since become emblematic of the tango itself – its notes the defining sound of the modern tango – from its first appearance to its flowering in the hands of virtuosi like Aníbal Troilo, Pedro Maffia and Ástor Piazzolla in later days. It is celebrated in famous tangos by Celedonio Flores, Pascual Contursi, Homero Manzi and this song by José González Castillo, father of the outstanding Cátulo Castillo.

> ¡Bandoneón! . . .
> Que lanzás al viento
> por tus cien heridas
> tu eterno lamento,
> y que en cada aliento
> renovás cien vidas
> ¡pa' gemir mejor! . . .
> ¡Sangrando armonías
> o llorando quedo,
> sos el fiel remedo
> de mi propio amor!
>
> Cuando se hinchan tus pulmones
> para volcar en mil sones
> el alma de tu armonía,

¡me parece la mía
tu doliente canción! . . .

Y te oprimo entre mis brazos
para arrancarla a pedazos
en una queja postrera,
¡como si en vos gimiera
mi propio corazón! . . .

¡Corazón! . . .
Que lanzás al viento
con cada suspiro
el hondo lamento
de tu sentimiento,
y en cada respiro
crece tu emoción . . .
Cuando en la tristeza
tu canción se abisma,
¡sos el alma misma
de mi bandoneón! . . .

Bandoneon / You cast to the wind / Through your hundred wounds / That eternal lament / And with each breath / You restore a hundred lives / To weep the better! / With the harmonies that bleed out from you / or the quiet tears / you are the faithful cure / for my own love!
When your lungs expand / and issue a thousand songs / the soul of your harmony / your sad song feels / like my very own . . .
And I squeeze you in my arms / to draw out the song little by little / in a long complaint / As if your sound / were the trembling of my own heart.
My heart! . . . / You cast into the wind / with every sigh / the deep feelings / of sorrow / and the emotion grows more intense / with

*every breath . . . / and when your song / sinks into sadness / you
are the very soul / of my bandoneon.*

('Bandoneón' – José González Castillo, n.d.)

The arrival of the bandoneon produced an immediate change
in the dance. The guitar and flute had accompanied the fast,
dramatic and erotic steps of the original dance – the 'ruffian's
dance' (the *tango rufianesco*).[7] Its frankly sexual gestures and
movements shocked and repelled the respectable middle clases,
yet they were not immune to the impact of the music, nor to its
seductions. The way in which the bandoneon was played added
drama and passion to the sound of tango, but it was slower and
more sensual, its undulations more melancholy and provocative.
And its arrival coincided with tango's first tentative steps towards
the new elegant cafés and cabarets around the well-lit streets of
the city centre, places like Lo de Hansen or El Velódromo, whose
names would soon appear in tango lyrics and circulate among
enthusiasts. The music itself began to become acceptable in the
more elegant, if slightly more liberal salons, though dancing was
still forbidden in most of them, and a new generation of performers
found audiences (and wages) beyond the barrio when they gave
exhibitions in the more adventurous venues. Rosendo Mendizábal
was an accomplished pianist whose 'El Entrerriano' became one
of the best known of the new tango concert pieces – music, in
other words, to be listened rather than danced to. Only the most
daring middle-class woman around 1900 would be prepared to
venture into the areas near the docks in the afternoon to seek out
the handsome young men who offered themselves as dance partners. But they could enthusiastically attend the exhibitions given
by the new generation of professional dancers, chief among them
Ovidio José Blanquet, known as 'El Cachafaz', 'the Insolent Kid'.

Tango was creeping across the border, or at least gaps had
been opened that allowed some communication between the two

El Cachafaz.

worlds of the city. The marginal quarters remained, from a middle-class point of view, places of danger and forbidden pleasure. And the estimated 20–30,000 prostitutes in Buenos Aires confirmed both the availability and the variety of the erotic. Traffic was, of course, predominantly one-way. If the women of the middle class approached in the afternoon light, their husbands slipped into the port area under cover of darkness. But tango's best known artists now made increasingly frequent incursions into the gleaming halls of the city centre. And in the theatres (attended by and large by the middle class) the world of tango began to be referred to in the comic operas (*sainetes*) and musicals (*zarzuelas*) that were popular at the time. It is true that the theatrical representation of the immigrant at the turn of the century was still largely comic, grotesque and caricatured – but tango music too was played in the same theatres. Though it might be publicly derided and reproved by the bourgeoisie, their fascinated response to its seductions made that rejection hypocritical at best.

Tango was making its way into the bourgeois world, albeit slowly and hesitantly. The rite of passage was largely completed during the first decade of the twentieth century. But it was a process fraught with contradictions. The numbers of immigrants had leapt once again in the 1890s, fuelling the anxieties of the middle classes. The growing working class was beginning to organize and forge the early trade unions, radical in their predominantly anarchist ideology and increasingly militant in their actions. The discontent at living and working conditions was rising, reaching a critical point in the 1907 rent strike in the *conventillos*, when, for the first time, the human beings pressed into the overcrowded shacks and shanties of the dock districts took on their landlords. It was commemorated in the *sainete* 'Los inquilinos' (The Tenants), which included a tango with the same title:

Señor intendente,
los inquilinos
se encuentran muy mal
se encuentran muy mal
pues los propietarios
o los encargados
nos quieren ahogar.
Abajo la usura
y abajo el abuso;
arriba el derecho
y arriba el derecho
del pobre también.

Mr Mayor / the tenants / are in a very bad way / in a very bad way / because the landlords / or their agents / are drowning us. / Down with usury / down with their abuses / long live justice / long live justice / and long live the rights / of poor people too.[8]

The inclusion of these issues in the popular music of the day testifies to the way in which the newly emerging tango lyrics had moved from the simply provocative or plainly obscene to becoming a narrative of the life and experience of the barrios – its housing, its resistance, its desires and frustrations, and to a very limited extent, its experience of work. It remained the voice of the barrios, its streets and communal life. And it retained as its central character the isolated young man, living the life of the streets, whose strutting and preening in the dance conceals a deeper sense of continuing marginality and exclusion.

As he protects himself with a facade of steps that demonstrate perfect control [the male tanguero] contemplates his absolute lack of control in the face of history and destiny.[9]

Women are very rarely heard in tango's early lyrics. There were some who made their name in this world despite their suppression – singers, dancers and madams. But it was always a dance led by men, danced with other men or women, but only very rarely by women with one another. The game of seduction it enshrined was not conducted between equals. When the first women tango singers emerged at the beginning of the Golden Age, they dressed in men's clothing.

But at this time, the majority of tango writers and musicians were part-time artists whose main source of income was elsewhere. Agustín Bardi worked in a shop, Vicente Greco sold newspapers, Juan Maglio was a mechanic – though they would later find an adequate living from tango. But first, tango would need to win the battle for acceptance.

And for that to happen, it had first to wrestle with the suspicion that tango still aroused and the very different visions of the dance.

The room fills with happy people; everywhere one hears phrases that could make a vigilante blush. In the background a group of petty criminals from the barrios with improvised disguises, in the theatre boxes handsome men and even more handsome girls. Suddenly the orchestra begins a tango and the couples begin to form. The china and compadre join together in a fraternal embrace, and then the dance begins, in which the dancers show such an art that it is impossible to describe the contortions, dodgings, impudent steps and clicking of the heels the tango causes.

The couples glide energetically to the beat of the dance, voluptuously, as if all their desires are placed in the dance. In the background, the people form groups to see figures done by a girl from the suburbs, who is proclaimed the mistress without rival in this difficult art, and the crowd applauds these prodigious figures, drawing back scandalized when the dancer's companion says 'Give me the pleasure, my little "china"'.[10]

The Scottish writer Robert Cunninghame Graham, however, seemed slightly more shocked by what he saw.

> They were so close to each other that the leg of the carefully pressed trouser would disappear in the tight skirt, the man holding her in such a close embrace that the hand ended up by the woman's face. They gyrated in a whirlwind, bending down to the floor, advancing the legs in front of each other while turning, all of this with a movement of the hips that seemed to fuse the impeccable trousers with the slitted skirt. The music continued more tumultuously, the musical times multiplied until, with a jump, the woman would throw herself into the arms of her partner, who would put her back on her feet.[11]

Clearly such antics would horrify the ladies of Palermo and reinforce their resistance to the tango's incursions into their lives. Conservative writers like Leopoldo Lugones and Manuel Galvez looked upon the tango with barely disguised racial arrogance: 'the product of cosmopolitanism, hybrid and ugly music . . . a grotesque dance . . . the embodiment of our national disarray'.[12] There were persistent attempts to close down the brothels, and eventually new ordinances to control the bordellos were passed in 1915. And the wealthy districts were becoming increasingly nervous about the rise of anarchist groups which they associated with prostitution and criminality.

In the end, their resistance was to no avail. Tango won its right to exist, but only after Tangomania hit Paris.

3 TANGO GOES TO PARIS

PLACES OF PLEASURE

At the Universal Exhibition of 1900, when Paris gathered the
products of the new and exciting modern world, from automobiles
to electricity, John Philip Sousa's band played ragtime music for
the middle class of Paris. Two years later, in 1902, 'Les Joyeux
Nègres' (The Cheerful Negroes), a show featuring The Little
Walkers at the Nouveau Cirque, caused a sensation when it
introduced the cakewalk to its audiences. In 1906, Debussy
composed his (unfortunately named) 'Gollywog's Cakewalk',
while in the following year Picasso and Matisse both produced
iconic paintings (*Les Desmoiselles d'Avignon* and *Blue Nude* respec-
tively) which celebrated the art of Africa, which they had seen
at the famous exhibition of African Art in Paris.

Earlier, as the Belle Époque reached its climax in 1900, a
younger Picasso was hurriedly sketching the clients and prostitutes
dancing at the clubs of Montmartre, just as Toulouse-Lautrec's
'Jane Avril' was appearing on advertising columns around the city,
thanks to the new techniques in colour printing. It was somehow
symbolic that the Moulin Rouge, built in 1885 as a windmill, should
be converted to a dance hall in 1900, when the famous red sails
came to signify not an advancing technology but a different aspect
of the new century – hedonism, sexuality and the pursuit of
pleasure. These places of entertainment advertised themselves as
refuges from the modern and the technological, as places where
the primitive and instinctual could find free and uncensored

expression. Paris, which Benjamin called 'the capital of the nine-teenth century',[1] was a place of exemplary order and impressive social control. Yet part of that order was the permitted existence of *lieux de plaisir* – 'places of pleasure' – on the margins of the city, behind the Wall in Montmartre and later in Montparnasse.

> From time immemorial, the rich society of Paris adopted a
> neutral space where all classes could rub shoulders, see each
> other, talk to each other, without making any more contact
> than the pursuit of pleasure demanded.[2]

And apart from talking and seeing, the bourgeois and the shopgirl or the demi-mondaine could dance the sensuous dances of this new age together. Dance manuals provided diagrams for urban Europeans on how to dance the cakewalk, just as, before the decade ended, classes and manuals would allow them to learn the tango.

While in Buenos Aires the contact between the outer, marginal areas and the modern city was limited to clandestine trips in the darkness, Paris was more liberal and perhaps less hypocritical in its pursuits of pleasure. Transgression lay across the boulevard, and the artists of the underworld, like Toulouse-Lautrec, were uninhibited in their representations of the diverse crowds of men gathering in the brothels and nightclubs. His portraits of the women, waiting for their customers and chatting desultorily, evoke people much like the 20–30,000 prostitutes gathered by then in Buenos Aires. In Buenos Aires, the first decade of the century saw the first cracks in the social barriers that had kept the Buenos Aires that saw itself as Paris apart from the marginal barrios and immigrant communities. But the full breakthrough would be made in the French capital itself.

There was a bizarre conjunction between a Paris that stood for the gamut of technological progress, as represented in the Great

Universal Exhibition of 1900, and its fascination with the primitive and the exotic. The exhibition itself erected circuses and performance spaces replete with symbols and images of the other distant world.[3] Paris was as fascinated by the machinery and technology, whose most glorious expression was the Métro, as it was by the colonial world, with its dark-skinned people and its echoes of the primitive. The Arab world concealed all that was mysterious and dangerous: Africa was the home of an uninhibited sexuality, the Far East was impenetrably (inscrutably) 'other'. And though Latin America remained more remote perhaps from France, the vision of the transatlantic world was equally distant from the civilized society of Paris, and equally exhilarating. The seduction of the primitive and the exotic was not exclusive to France, of course – but it was intensified there in social and sexual mores.[4]

There were meeting points between those two worlds, crossroads where the primitive and the modern met and co-existed uneasily for the briefest of moments. In France the archetypal place of encounter was in Marseilles, where ships brought Africa, Asia and the Americas to the very threshold of the most advanced modern world. It was the underworld of the port that was the birthplace of the Apache Dance,[5] which became a craze as the twentieth century began. One or two men, usually dressed in the sailor's striped *maillot*, danced with a woman in a brothel or a café – the clear implication was that one was a pimp and the other a customer, or perhaps a lover, and she a prostitute. The dance was dramatic, violent and acrobatic – a representation of the violence of men against women. When two men were shown battling over the woman, she was thrown between them, hurled across the floor, spun in the air. The new craze spread rapidly to Paris, where it was given its name by a newspaper reporter who, after watching a gang fight outside the Sacre Cœur cathedral, likened them to warring Apache Indians. It had little to do with any knowledge or understanding of this particular group

– rather he was using the word 'Apache' as a symbol of the primitive and the uncivilized. The gangs of Paris seized the definition and appropriated it for themselves.

It was brutal and acrobatic, yet it was also a couple dance imbued with a kind of violent eroticism. It was the theme of a short 1902 silent film called *A Tough Dance*, with Kid Foley and Sailor Lil, and two years later Joseph Smith took the dance to New York. It emerged very quickly from the shadows into mainstream Parisian life, albeit on the other side of the boulevard. The famous and influential dance teacher Maurice Mouvet created his own version of the dance at the Café de Paris in 1907, and two years later Mistinguett, who dominated the world of dance in France for many years, danced this first 'tough couple dance' at the iconic Moulin Rouge.

Others came through Marseilles too. Manuel Pizarro, a musician, landed there in 1900 and made his way to Paris, where he found a room at the Hôtel Pigalle in Montmartre. Meeting a friend there, he joined the musicians at the Princesse. Meanwhile, when the frigate *Sarmiento* docked at the southern port,[6] the crew took to the local taverns and cafés the sheet music for some of the tangos popular in the port of Buenos Aires. They played Ángel Villoldo's 'El Choclo' and 'La Morocha', both popular pieces in La Boca and Nueva Pompeya, from which many of the sailors would have come.

But by this time, tango was not entirely new. Pizarro and his friends were already playing at the Princesse, tango had been seen on film for the first time in 1900, and Giraudet, a much respected dance teacher in Paris, had begun to teach it. Erotic dance was nothing new, of course; the Moulin Rouge was renowned for its cancan, a much bawdier overtly sexual version than the one most of us have become familiar with. The Apache dance itself, behind its dramatic violent content, was a dance charged with eroticism. And the excitement around tango had as much to do with its origins in the Argentinian underworld and its suggestive gestures as with a confused notion of a primitive world of cowboys and open prairies.

In 1907, Alfredo Gobbi and Flora Rodríguez, already famous in Buenos Aires, arrived in Paris, where they remained for seven years, feeding the tango frenzy. The popular fascination with the dance was inadvertently inflamed by the visit of the Argentine president Julio Roca in that same year, and by the comments of his ambassador in France, Enrique Rodríguez Larreta.

> In Buenos Aires, tango is found only in whorehouses and filthy taverns. It is never danced in the respectable lounges, nor between civilized men and women, for tango is crude to the ear of any Argentine worthy of his nation.[7]

If Larreta's intention was to shock or frighten off the Parisian middle class, he failed signally. Tango was exciting precisely because of its exotic foreign origin!

> For the public of Paris or London, tango is no more than a vaguely sinful, exotic dance and they dance it because of its sensual, perverse elements and because it is somewhat barbaric.[8]

Tango rapidly took the place of the Apache in the nightclubs of Montmartre, or Montparnasse, which was rapidly becoming de rigueur for lovers of nightlife. Picasso, Matisse and all the young artists congregated there and shared with the liberal bourgeois public a love of things sensual and primitive. The collections of erotic photos of the era show naked women in classical poses against backgrounds of Roman vases and painted landscape; but they also contain a high proportion of photographs of nubile young African and Arab women in pornographic poses.

The Exhibition of African Art caused a sensation in the Paris of 1905, and inspired a wide range of artworks, among them Picasso's *Desmoiselles d'Avignon*. And Diaghilev's Ballets Russes reflected the new fashion in its scenography, its costumes and its choreography.

> We might suspect that the choreography was adapted to Parisian taste, to the 'dances brunes' (brown dances), the Apaches and the bals musette. Given people's boredom with the waltz and the quadrille, a kind of convulsive and sensual new waltz was invented which evoked a fantasy Buenos Aires, a mix of Shanghai and Chicago.[9]

The impression was probably encouraged by the 4,000 or so Argentines living in Paris who introduced tango to Paris in this first decade of the century. But there were also growing numbers of tango musicians, dancers and singers there, many of whom were first or (by now) second generation immigrants. There is disagreement over when and where the tango was first danced in Paris. What is certainly true is that it was popular on both sides of the Atlantic by 1906 or 1907, and that by 1913 it had taken Paris, London and New York by storm. Argentine musicians were arriving in Paris in numbers now, partly because of tango's popularity and partly to make the first recordings, since Buenos Aires had no recording facilities as yet. The majority of visiting Argentines, however, were the young scions of the wealthy urban classes for whom a stay in Paris was an obligatory part of their social education. They had already paid clandestine visits to the brothels and cafés of La Boca and the working-class districts before they left – and in Paris they could practise their new-found techniques in a far more open way. The Apache dances that they witnessed in the *boîtes* of Paris seemed very like the tango – and their European fellows seemed thirsty for any physical expression that smacked of primitive places and forbidden desires.

If it was sailors who brought the sheet music to Paris, and the musicians of the bordellos who first took their instruments to play there, it was the Argentine aristocracy and its Parisian confrères who took up the tango with the greatest enthusiasm. Ricardo Güiraldes, a writer from an Argentine landowning family, who was in Paris in 1910, attended all the parties in the palaces of the aristocracy: he demonstrated the daring new dance at a ball held by Madame de Reszke and the Princess Murat. 'Do we dance this standing up?', the Princess asked. The tango's dramatic sensuality clearly excited the wealthy friends of Güiraldes and his friend Jorge Newbery, son of another of Argentina's wealthiest families and, like Güiraldes, a good dancer. Güiraldes's poem 'Tango' was written in that year:[10]

> *Creator of silhouettes that glide by silently*
> *as if hypnotized by a blood-filled dream,*
> *hats tilted over sardonic sneers.*
> *The all-absorbing love of a tyrant,*
> *jealously guarding his dominion*
> *over women who have surrendered submissively,*
> *like obedient beasts . . .*
> *Sad, severe tango . . .*
> *Dance of love and death . . .*

Güiraldes's famous novel, *Don Segundo Sombra* (1926),[11] was a romantic recreation of *gaucho* life which established for his own class and their European friends the myth of a mysterious and primitive Argentina.

Tango bands were already playing in the clubs of Paris and London, though in Paris local rules obliged them to dress in national costume, in the uniform of the rural *gaucho*, which, in the context of Paris, served only to emphasize its exoticism. These *orquestas típicas* played in nightclubs and at the afternoon *thés dansants* where the ladies of the middle and upper classes could dance with their chauffeurs and hairdressers. Casimiro Aín had been dancing since 1904 and gave classes to men and women, among them the young Rudolph Valentino, who would later become Hollywood's favourite tango dancer and archetypal Latin seducer.

It was Josephine Baker's pastiche of African dance and her spectacular erotic shows that summarized the era. But Jean Cocteau described the atmosphere with a more jaundiced eye:

> It was 1913. Soto and his cousin Manolo Martínez had brought Argentine tango on a gramophone. They lived in a little hotel in Montmorency. You could see old ladies who had never left home before and young rebellious women from the upper classes. Old and young danced pressed against Soto and Martinez. . . . The whole city was dancing the tango, whose steps at that time were very complicated. Fat men walked with grave expressions, marking the rhythm, stopping on one leg and lifting the other like a dog about to urinate, showing the soles of their shiny patent shoes. They pasted down their hair with Argentine 'gomina'. Age didn't matter. Everyone tangoed.[12]

This was 1912. By the following year, the craze for tango had engulfed everything – much to the distress of the Archbishop of Paris who said 'We condemn the dance imported from abroad known by the name of tango which, by its nature, is indecent and offensive to morals . . .'.

And the Kaiser forbade any member of the armed forces to dance to this scandalous rhythm while wearing their uniform. In the following year, President Poincaré banned the tango at the Élysée Palace. But it was all to no avail; none of the condemnations had the slightest effect. Tango had begun in the shadowy barrios of Buenos Aires, it had taken ship to Paris and from there spread at extraordinary speed across a world living through the fragile pre-war years in a kind of endless carpe diem – eating, drinking and making merry, for tomorrow we die.

The craze had crossed the Channel and the Atlantic and had moved east through Europe. In February 1911, the *New York Times* announced: 'Some steps of a new dance called the Tango Illustrated'.[13] There were equal numbers of articles condemning tango for its overt and provocative sensuality, but the *thés dansants* had taken root there among the ladies of the middle class. In 1913, dance teacher Gladys Beattie Crozier wrote airily about the '*Thé Dansant* clubs which have sprung up all over the West End of London', where one could enjoy 'a most elaborate and delicious tea served within a moment of one's arrival, while listening to an excellent string band playing delicious, haunting Tango airs, with an occasional waltz or lively rag-time melody . . .'.[14] In Fulham, tango could be danced with accompanying fish and chips![15]

In the United States, formal dance was dominated by the elegant brother and sister team Vernon and Irene Castle. They had become hugely wealthy by exploiting the dance craze, opening dance centres and academies, giving exhibitions and publishing dance instruction manuals. The popularity of dance and the frantic search for novelty had produced a list of new forms in the first decade of the twentieth century. The older dances, like the schottische or the waltz, were supplanted by other more vigorous, wilder forms like the maxixe, the cakewalk and later variants like the turkey-trot and other animal imitations. The tango, of course, was less athletic and more sexual – but the twisting of bodies and the obvious erotic references, which did not seem to disturb the French at all, proved too much for the transatlantic public. And the tango in any case was changing – perhaps in preparation for its triumphant return home.

In Paris, the tango was at the heart of an exploration of sensuality and eroticism, albeit restrained by middle-class mores. But its stars were as sensual as the two dominant figures of the cabarets –

Mistinguett and Josephine Baker. Cabaret was a spectacle, a theatrical drama that on a smaller scale could be re-enacted on the dance floor with a greater or lesser degree of physical contact and erotic simulation. In a sense, as it developed, tango moved between the *rufianesco* – the pimp's enactment of sexual pleasure and the battle between men for the attention of the prostitute – and *romántico*, in which those initial gyrations had been stylized and dramatized.[16] In these early years of the twentieth century, as it travelled the world, tango moved between these two expressions.

In the French capital, the memory of the Apache dance conserved that feeling of the underworld and a struggle for power between men and women. Among the early pupils there was the young Rudolph Valentino, whose tango in the *Four Horsemen of the Apocalypse* not only launched him into the realms of superstardom but also created an iconic image of the dance itself. As described by Marta Savigliano, Valentino's version is closer to the Apache dance or the *valse chaloupé* that Mistinguett presented before her public. The scene is 'the famous Boca quarter of Buenos Aires'. Valentino, dressed as a *gaucho*, complete with riding crop, watches Beatrice Domínguez dancing with a man she clearly does not like. He pushes him away and Valentino and Domínguez enter the frame.

> After some individual gyrations, their hands join and they move around the dance floor performing smooth glides, controlled dips and slow sensuous swayings. Finally they embrace too closely and she breaks into contortions attempting to avoid a kiss that he insistently seeks. Unable to satisfy his desire, Valentino pushes her away with violence. She lands on the floor and drags herself to his feet in an ambivalent gesture of hatred and rapture. In the end he resorts to his secret weapon, his *boleadoras*, . . . and lassoes her.

It is the perfect machista ritual.

The journey to London, and from there to New York, softened and modified the element of erotic confrontation. The dance craze in Britain was tied to a notion of 'social dancing', with its emphasis on etiquette, refined social conduct and a properly prepared environment – as set out in Gladys Beattie Crozier's manual *The Tango and How to Do It* (1913). By 1913, the instruction manuals were proliferating and exhibition dancing on both sides of the Atlantic became a profitable pursuit. And the influence of tango was not limited to the dance itself. Fashion acknowledged the demand for freer movement for women, boned corsets were replaced by more flexible basques, and lightweight fabrics were

'La Rumba' poster.

introduced which both permitted ease of movement and emphasized the sensuality and fluidity of the dancer. Orange, the colour
of tango, became dominant and new dishes claimed their origins
in tango.[17]

The dance that had celebrated its origins in the sexual underworld and the primitive rural world, exemplified in dress and
gesture, was giving way to the romantic version on the one hand,
and on the other to dance as a sport. The sensual movements of
the original became athletic actions instead, and the embrace
gradually returned to the formal distance between the partners
that had been closed in the body contact that had so taken aback
the Scottish writer Robert Cunninghame Grahame.

> As they walked through the passages, men pressed close
> up to women and murmured in their ears, telling them
> anecdotes that made them flush and giggle, as they protested
> in an unprotesting style. Those were the days of the first
> advent of the Tango Argentino, the dance that has since
> circled the whole world, as it were, in a movement of the
> hips. Ladies pronounced it charming as they half closed their
> eyes and let a little shiver run across their lips. Men said that
> it was the only dance worth dancing. It was so Spanish, so
> unconventional, and combined all the aesthetic movements
> of the figures on an Etruscan vase with the strange grace of
> Hungarian gypsies . . . it was, one may say, so . . . as you may
> say . . . you know.[18]

It was under this conservative Anglo-Saxon influence that
tango became a social dance, and increasingly a kind of sport
where athleticism prevailed over sensual expression. There were
international competitions, and – after a struggle – the dance was
redefined. It was now no longer 'Latin', with all the exotic implications of the word, but 'modern', incorporated into the world of

contemporary ballroom dancing, with its rapidly accumulating rules and regulations. The interweaving of limbs should now occur only symbolically and at a distance – as the dance manuals of Vernon and Irene Castle made very clear.

The music was changing too, in response to the twin impact of tango's globalization and the expansion of its clientele into the bourgeois centres of the world's great cities. The fast *milonga* had given way to the slower more dramatic expression encouraged by the bandoneon. In Paris, the '*Orquesta típica*' dressed in national dress to play for the dancers. By 1913, however, the ensembles were growing, adding extra bandoneons and strings, and their dress was changing too. Dinner jackets reflected the tango's entry into the elegant world of the French bourgeoisie, but they in turn responded to the exoticism and excitement of the dance. At the same time, the dance was re-choreographed. While Stravinsky's *The Rite of Spring* still resonated with a self-conscious primitivism, Grossmith and Dare's hit 1916 musical *The Sunshine Girl* featured a tango considerably less daring than its original.[19]

Paris tango in 1913.

The first generation of tango musicians, dancers and singers were often workers who played at night in the brothels and cafés. In Paris, they changed their mode of dress and became professionals. Few of these early musicians had musical training – Rosendo Mendizábal was an important exception – but they began to commit their songs to paper as the new century opened, humming or whistling their tunes for others to set them down. Eduardo Arolas, a renowned bandoneon player, was among the first tango lyricists, as improvised words gave way to written lyrics. His tango 'Una noche de garufa' (1909), with words by Gabriel Clausi, vies for a place as the first tango with lyrics.

En esta noche de garufa yo me quiero divertir
con los amigos
de bohemia en el viejo Armenonville.
La vida es corta y se
pianta muy pronto,
en esta noche hay que vivir.
En las nostálgicas veladas
vuelve el tiempo del ayer
con este tango que nos lleva
como un sueño a su compás.
Viejos recuerdos, paicas papusas,
dulce momento del ayer.
Cómo me emocionan tus notas
en esta velada porteña,
deja que la música embriague
para hacer, del tango una fiesta.

On this night of pleasure I will take it where I can / With my
Bohemian friends in the old Armenonville. / Life is short and ends
all too soon / So this night is for living. / In those nostalgic parties /
Yesterday returns / With the tango that carries us / into a dream

with its rhythm / Old memories, beautiful women we loved /
Sweet moments in the past. / The music moves me so in this
Buenos Aires night / Let the music intoxicate you / And let the
tango / turn the night into a celebration.
  ('Una noche de garufa', A night of pleasure – Eduardo Arolas, 1909)

Arolas went to Paris in 1919, and died there in mysterious
circumstances in 1924. He was 32 years old. His story was repeated
among the young men and women who pursued the dream of
Paris. Nearly all the musicians and performers emerged from urban
poverty in Argentina; most died in very similar circumstances. In
1913, it was reported that over 100 Argentine, musicians, singers
and dancers flocked to Paris; few made a living.

The tango craze which they hoped to benefit from had two
very different expressions. On stage and in revue, tango retained
its powerful exotic charge and its sexuality. But in the dance salons,
the tango followed new rules established by dance masters like the
Castles in the u.s. or M. André de Fouquières in Paris.[20]

The original choreography had been stylized into glamorous,
almost balletic, postures (extended arms, stretched torsos and
necks, light feet) and rough apache-like figures (deep dips,
backward bends, dizzying sways) with matching walks in
between . . . The basic continental tango was glamorised on
the stages and tamed in the ballrooms . . . the music was
especially composed so as to be exotically languid and retained
only some of its rhythm.[21]

For those Argentines who found themselves in Europe or the
United States, there was little alternative but to act out Western
fantasies of Argentine life. As Buenos Aires was rapidly becoming
one of the world's largest cities, its urban culture was being
represented in *gaucho* costume and rural backdrops. In the u.s.,

tango had also changed in deference to the sensibilities of the middle classes. The Castles emphasized elegance and pattern in the dance, and held the partners in a safely distant embrace. When the wealthy Mrs Stuyvesant wanted a tango for her salon, but baulked at the sensuality of it, the Castles conceived the 'Innovation' whose distinguishing feature was that the partners did not touch! The Castles went to some lengths to tame and colonize, describing the tango in their influential *Modern Dance* of 1914 thus:

> The much-misunderstood Tango becomes an evolution of the eighteenth century Minuet . . . when the Tango degenerates into an acrobatic display or into salacious sensation it is the fault of the dancers and not of the dance. The Castle tango is courtly and artistic.[22]

The tango musicians and dancers who were seeking their fortune in Europe and the United States would have had considerable difficulty in accepting that. Indeed, despite the fact that the Victor label in the u.s. and Odeon in Europe were successfully recording some of these artists, in the United States the music was attenuated and adapted to the local morality, and the more popular lyrics were those written by local writers who often translated exoticism into the absurdity of the novelty song.

> *When the great big Dip Dip Dip Dipper*
> *Did the Tango in the sky*
> *He told them all the merry news*
> *As he went rolling by.*
> *Then he called on Jupiter Pluvius*
> *For his orchestra to play*
> *And the Price of admission to this wonderful dance,*
> *Was a tiny silv'ry ray . . .*[23]

Rudolph Valentino.

Storm Roberts notes, for example, that a very large proportion of the Latin music recorded in the 1910s and early 1920s seems to have been laid down by a group called the International Novelty Orchestra.[24]

75

The Parisian Tango Malouze.

Others did place the stress on the athleticism of the dance movements. Ted Shawn and Ruth St Denis were early exponents of tango as well as a range of other exotic dances that were heavily Americanized versions of dances from India and Africa; their own vision of tango included backdrops to match. Clearly the burgeoning film industry was a powerful influence on the interpretation of dance. And Valentino's famous performance in the 1921 film *Four Horsemen of the Apocalypse* was a reflection of the already hugely popular *thés dansants* of New York. Valentino himself was a dancer for hire (or a gigolo) at Bustanoby's Domino Room on 39th and 6th.

But the rhythms of tango permeated the other emerging music of the era, from blues to jazz. And it was clearly the youthful grandparent of the Charleston and Black Bottom of the 1920s.

TANGO COMES HOME

Many of the Argentines who had flocked to Paris, whether the gilded youth on their own version of the Grand Tour, or the working-class tango musicians and performers who had responded to the tangomania that took hold of the city on the eve of war, returned to Argentina at the start of the First World War.

In fact, tango was becoming acceptable even before the exiles returned. The party organized by the Baron de Marchi, an Italian aristocrat living in Buenos Aires, in the Palais de Glace in late 1912 was a turning point, and he continued to organize 'several aristocratic tango events (in private mansions, restaurants and clubs) to openly bring his high-life acquaintances into contact with skilful *tangueros*'.[25] Those young bloods who had made the obligatory trip to Paris were prominent guests at these affairs, of course.

In this time of transition, the tango orchestras too were changing in manner and style, as well as in their instrumental line-up. Those who had remained in Buenos Aires still used the underground pseudonyms that betrayed their origins in the slums and *conventillos* – El Tuerto ('the One-eyed man'), El Chivo ('the Goat'), El Rusito ('the Little Russian'), and so on. And the life the early tangos celebrated was crowded with petty criminals and toughs, pimps and con men still. Most of them had learned their music by ear. And unlike the tango orchestras of Paris, the musicians of Buenos Aires in this first decade limited their ensembles to piano, bandoneon and violin (like Francisco Canaro's trio), or the guitar, flute, bandoneon and violin of Juan Maglio's band (formed in 1912).[26]

The proliferating cafés and cabarets of the city centre were evidence of how significant the European seal of approval was.

The Café Royale and the Pigalle were among the most sought-after locales. Argentina's gilded youth would spill out of Madame Jeanne's high-class brothel into the Armenonville Cabaret. There they could dance to the music of the icons of what became known as *La Guardia Vieja* – 'the Old Guard' of tango musicians who still wore their origins on their sleeves, albeit sleeves that were increasingly well tailored to reflect the elegant surroundings in which the musicians were now placed. The orchestras were still playing for dancing; the emerging group of lyricists were still a minority and their songs basically interludes in the evening's (and morning's) dance.

The bandleaders of the epoch also wrote ballads – Roberto Firpo produced 'El compinche' and 'La chola', Juan Maglio 'El Zurdo' and Vicente Greco's output included 'La infanta' and 'El Pibe'. And among the singers were a first generation of women whose heyday would come in the 1920s.

The tango was changing – and so was the city of its birth. The immigrant's song was about to become the ballad of the city. And within a short time, the expression of the nation itself.

> Foreign/superior recognition empowered the tango – which had been a locally denigrated cultural expression – and made it a competitive marker of national identity.[27]

It is profoundly ironic that the process of assimilation and acceptance that made the forging of a new national identity possible should have begun in Europe. In fact, as will become clear, it was a complex business. During and after the First World War, tango became an international phenomenon, a dance of local origins made universal. At the same time, within Argentina, it became a symbolic expression of a social process whereby the immigrants – physically and psychologically marginalized for nearly forty years – were absorbed into the mainstream of Argentina, or more

TANGO GOES TO PARIS

particularly, Buenos Aires society. This was not to say that the social divisions had in any sense disappeared; the ruling class remained resolutely *criollo*, of Spanish origin, and held itself physically apart in its well-defined upper-class districts. The children and grandchildren of the immigrants were still to be found in the working-class areas. But their music could be heard, and danced to, everywhere. And more importantly, tango was now also song, expressing nostalgia for a recreated (and romanticized) *arrabal* and more general existential positions which found their definition in the *lunfardo* terms that survived into the language – like the omnipresent *mufarse* – a kind of moping or melancholy reflection which some writers insist is particularly characteristic of Argentines.

Tango had certainly broken out of the barrio – but it remained at its heart the expression of an urban experience of solitude, of nostalgia and loss.

Del ciego musicante la música manida,
la tonada gangosa de un lejano acordeón
revive en una estampa borrosa y desvaída
el alma arrabalera del turbio callejón.
La muchacha modista que cegó una quimera
dorada, que no pudo jamás satisfacer,
flor que duró tan sólo lo que una primavera
y pasó como todo lo que no ha de volver.

Qué profunda tristeza
tiene la calle sola.
La música lejana
solloza una milonga.
Todo está como entonces,
cuando tú eras la novia
que gustaba los versos,
los besos y las rosas . . .

Yo también como tú me perdí en el camino
y entre sombras extrañas paseo mi tristeza
y no le pido cuentas de mi vida al destino,
aunque es larga la ruta y ruda la maleza.
El mismo torbellino nos lleva al mismo puerto,
la misma sed de olvido nos une en hermandad.
Qué lejos nuestras almas del callejón desierto
donde la vida un día nos vino a despertar.

The music coming from the blind musician / the seductive tune
Of a distant accordion / brings back a blurred and shifting image /
the soul of the barrio and the murky alleyway. / The young seam-
stress blinded by a golden / chimera, that she could never satisfy /
a flower that lasted only a single spring / and passed like all things
that never will return.
How deep the sadness / of the empty street / the distant music /
Sobs a milonga. / It's all like it was / when you were the lover /
Who enjoyed poetry / kisses and flowers . . . / Like you I got lost on
the way / and now I carry my sadness through strange shadows/
and I don't ask fate for explanations of my life / though the road is
long and the going tough. / The same storm will carry us to the
same harbor / And we are joined by the same yearning to forget.

('Yo también como tú', Me too, just like you
– Diego Larriera Varela, 1926)

4 TANGO FINDS ITS VOICE

TRANSITIONS

While its wealthier young people were sowing their wild oats in Paris and elsewhere, a restless Buenos Aires was relentlessly moving on. The changes were physical, social and cultural; and it was finding new political forms too. In 1912, the Sáenz Peña Law marked a key moment of transition. The rent strikes in the *conventillos* in 1907 involved 120,000 people and announced a change in the attitudes of their immigrant inhabitants. The cowering new arrival, fearful of the landlord and his agents and powerless in the face of them, grew taller as the twentieth century began. By now, their insecure status as immigrants was changing; their sons and daughters were citizens of the new Argentina and they and their families now made up a significant majority of the urban population, reaching 50 per cent by 1914.

By 1914, the total population of Argentina was close to 8 million, 3 million of them immigrants, living mostly in the cities and principally in Buenos Aires. In two decades the number of industrial workers had doubled, and the overwhelming majority of them were foreign immigrants who had arrived in the last two decades of the previous century. There were 100 engineering factories employing around 15,000 workers but over 2000 plants of every kind, two-thirds of them owned by foreign entrepreneurs. And this industrial growth was helped by a level of external capital that made Argentina the recipient of the largest volume of external investment in the world in the years to 1913.

If the immigrant populations were occupying an increasingly central role in modern Argentina, this working-class majority remained marginalized, both socially and physically, and exploited. But the social relations of production were changing. The rent strikes were signs of a new sense of the collective, of burgeoning forms of organization. A new generation of trade unions was emerging informed by the ideas of anarchism and socialism that the European migrants had brought with them. The new unions were general unions organizing the unskilled – the new sector of the working class that was denied access to the tighter and more exclusive guild organizations of an earlier generation. And with them came a growing confidence in the right of immigrant workers to play their role in the new Argentine nation, a nation reforming in a cosmopolitan, modernizing image. The Sáenz Peña Law of 1912 was a recognition of the expanding nation and the demands of its new citizens to participate fully in it.

> After 1900, a militant Anarchist movement established a large following among the immigrant workers in Buenos Aires. There was a series of violent general strikes, which triggered a spate of repressive measures by the government. Strikes were broken by force and legislation was passed by congress allowing the government to deport or imprison working class leaders.[1]

In 1902, the Congress passed the Law of Residence, which allowed rights of residence to be withdrawn in the case of 'undesirables'. In 1910, this was reinforced by the more openly repressive Law of Social Defence. Social conflict was clearly intensifying, and the influence of anarchism, with its disregard for the struggle to win control of the state and its emphasis on direct collective action, connected with the experience of immigrant workers and their families. The rent strike of 1907 was a clear expression of a political philosophy that linked social and trade union struggles. And it was not surprising that anarchist ideas should take hold in an environment in which political control remained in the hands of the old landowning oligarchy, while the economic and social transformation of the country was occurring in the cities.

While the working class was developing forms of collective organization to fight back against its marginalization and exclusion, the middle class was also growing increasingly restive with a political system still dominated by the old elite. They were enjoying economic prosperity and profiting from growth, yet they remained marginal to the political process. Their frustration was expressed by the Radical Party.

> Radical doctrine and ideology . . . were little more than an eclectic and moralistic attack on the oligarchy, to which was appended the demand for the introduction of representative government.[2]

The Radicals had to achieve a delicate balancing act between the oligarchy on the one hand and an increasingly angry and militant working class on the other.

Sáenz Peña's Law of 1912, passed just two years after the promulgation of the Law of Social Defence, had a clear objective: to channel political dissent towards parliamentary democracy and away from the violent revolutionary rhetoric which was becoming increasingly strident as the first decade of the century ended. The Radical Party itself had often employed a vague revolutionary language in its early years. Yet it was equally ill at ease with the multilingual voices of protest growing louder in the barrios of Buenos Aires. Sáenz Peña's commitment was to offer the Radical Party a stake in the existing, but reformed political system – as it was very clear that in an election in which the middle classes voted, their majority support would go to the Radicals and their leader, and presidential candidate, Hipólito Irigoyen.

Irigoyen was elected in 1916; his rise to the presidency marked the end of a century-old political system controlled by the old elite and used to maintain its interests. They remained the controlling economic class, of course, but the shifting and changing balance of power between these two social forces would mark and shape the subsequent two decades of Argentine political life. The Radicals, even before their election to the national government, had consolidated their influence at local and regional levels, in particular in the growing cities where the networks they created felt and looked very like the system of controlling city bosses that was already well established in the United States. For the working class, however, the changes were limited, and what improvements were achieved were the result of militant trade union action. While the immigrant populations may well have thrown their support behind the Radicals and against the old ruling class, their relationship with a Radical party in power remained tense and conflictive.[3]

POLITICS AND CULTURE

After its boom years on both sides of the Atlantic, tango came home in 1914 as the exiles returned. They came flushed with their success in the cafés and clubs of the demi-monde of Paris and their acceptance in the elegant salons of the city. Those who returned from the United States brought back a different, sexually less adventurous tango, its steps sacrificed in exchange for access to the *thés dansants* of the Upper East Side and the elegant parties of the *grandes dames* of New York. What they found in Buenos Aires was that news of Europe's craze for tango had arrived before them, and that new cabarets and cafés had opened in the city centre, bearing French names and European decor. The Armenonville and the Pigalle, Lo de Hansen or the Café Tortini mimicked a kind of French grand style. There was little here to recall the rural interior from which the internal migrants had come nor to reflect the poor rural background from which the steerage passengers on the migrant ships had emerged.

The beginning of the First World War brought the exiles back to the River Plate. But tango had arrived back before them. Though it was still seen as risqué, tango could now be danced in Buenos Aires at semi-respectable tea dances, where the more adventurous ladies of the middle class partnered the slick young gigolos who frequented the cafés of the city centre in the afternoons. In the evenings their husbands would dance with women who were definitely not of their social circle, but young women who had graduated from the brothels and cabarets of the port areas to the grander surroundings of the new cafés. The resentment of their erstwhile pimps, the *compadritos*, when they had to watch their charges disappear into this other world on the arm of a wealthy protector (the *bacán*) would be a central theme of the tango songs of subsequent decades.

> *Muchacho*
> *Que porque la suerte quiso*
> *Vivís en un primer piso*
> *De un palacete central,*
> *Que para vicios y placeres*
> *Para farras y mujeres*
> *Dispones de un capital.*
>
> *Muchacho*
> *Que no sabes el encanto*
> *De haber derramado llanto*
> *Por un amor de mujer,*
> *Que no sabes qué es secarse*

En una timba y armarse
Para volverse a meter . . .

Young man / who because destiny placed you / in a first-floor apart-
ment / in a mansion in the centre of town / and for vices and pleas-
ures / for parties and women / gave you money to spare.
Young man / you don't know the enchantment / of weeping tears /
for the love of a woman / who doesn't know what it's like / to be
cleaned out in a game and steel yourself / to go back the next day
and start again . . .

          ('Muchacho', Young Man – Celedonio Flores, 1929)

Another irony of the triumphant return of tango from
Europe was that the tango recordings that were causing such an
impact in the wider world were largely made in Europe and the
United States, mainly on the Odeon and the Victor labels, respec-
tively. There were some recordings being made in Buenos Aires,
but they signally failed to capture the spirit of tango as the French
and German engineers had done.

> The (local) gramophone companies did not aim their product
> at those who would rather spend their money on sex, narcotics
> and pistols. Early examples of Tango are largely stiff, somewhat
> ersatz affairs and the few genuine groups to record made little
> impact on the domestic market.[4]

The Odeon label's agent in Buenos Aires, Max Glücksmann,
was instrumental in reacquainting Argentina with the music of
its lower depths. Odeon, a German company, preferred to have
Germans selling their products abroad, and Glücksmann was
appointed their agent in Buenos Aires. As the war affected supplies
of shellac and made the transport of discs more difficult, the ties
between headquarters and its far-flung agencies were broken.

Glücksmann, who was already active in finding and recording local artists, persuaded his bosses to provide both a pressing plant and a recording engineer in Buenos Aires. He went on signing up artists and performers, who now appeared on his own label, 'Discos Nacional'. At war's end, Glücksmann reached an agreement with his old employer and his records began to be exported back to Europe, where they caught the mood of the 'Jazz Age'.

The *Vieja Guardia*, or 'Old Guard' as this first generation of tango musicians and performers were called, developed in Paris. It was there that the original tango trios expanded into sextets, like the early *orquestas típicas* of Juan Maglio and Vicente Greco. Tangomania was providing opportunities for tango musicians to live from their music. And the dance was also changing under the influence of Europe and America. The fast, tripping style (conserved most closely in the *milonga* today) was giving way to the slower, more dramatic and less crudely erotic version – the *tango argentino*. And that in turn eased its entry into the respectable night life of Argentina's bourgeoisie, and opened a new market for the enterprising Glücksmann.

Under Glücksmann's tutelage another change was taking place, more profound and far-reaching, and moved by a combination of transformations. The Law of Social Defence of 1910 had referred explicitly to social and political undesirables whose right to remain in Argentina could be withdrawn. It seemed a dramatic reversal of that original assurance of four decades earlier that immigrants could become part of the expanding Argentine nation.

The target was clearly not so much the immigrant community as such as the militants and dissidents who had begun to stamp their presence on the society through acts of political violence in some cases, and more generally through the growing trade union movement whose dominant anarchist ideology made it less amenable to political negotiation.

At first sight, the decision to withdraw the legal recognition of brothels may seem to be unconnected. But 'from 1900 onwards prostitutes were linked symbolically to the most dangerous men in Argentina – the anarchists'.[5] And the association of tango with the sexual underworld was explicit.

Yet if sexual commerce became less visible and less tolerated, its most fervid expression simply stepped across the lines of class and the physical frontiers between urban barrios and made its way into the wider world. It was helped by Glücksmann's energetic support for the genre, of course, as well as by the advent of radio, though sheet music continued to be sold in large quantities well into the 1930s too.

But perhaps the most active guarantee of tango's survival was the emergence of a new form – tango-song and its particular poetry. Although there were already recognized lyricists in the tango world, most notably Ángel Villoldo, tango remained a music for dancing. Yet by 1917–18, the lyrics were beginning to become as well known and as enthusiastically received as its music. Tango had found a voice.

THE SINGERS AND THE SONGS

Pascual Contursi's 'Mi noche triste' (My sad night), written in 1917, was not the first tango with words. 'Dame la lata' was written in the 1880s and by the following decade verses proliferated – but they were, like the early blues, largely invitations to sex couched in not very subtle metaphors: 'Touch me the way I like it', 'Shake my curtains', and many others like them. The early twentieth century produced the first lyricists, particularly Ángel Villoldo, who injected some social comment into these early songs, as in his 'El carrero y el cochero' (The carter and the coachman) and the emblematic 'El porteñito' of 1903. But his most famous tango, 'El Choclo' only acquired lyrics some two decades after its first publication in 1910.

'Mi noche triste' is universally acknowledged as the first of a new genre, the *tango-canción* or tango-song. Its accompaniment was the music of the *Vieja Guardia* of Roberto Firpo and Vicente Greco whose expanded ensembles still played for dancing. But by 1917, tango was becoming familiar and ubiquitous in Buenos Aires, as the sounds emerging from the elegant cabarets echoed the music of the street organs that had taken tango to the pavements of the city.

> *Al paso tardo de un pobre viejo*
> *Puebla de notas el arrabal,*
> *Con un concepto de vidrios rotos*
> *El organito crepuscular.*
> *Dándole vueltas a la manija*
> *Un hombre rengo marcha detrás,*
> *Mientras la dura pata de palo*
> *Marca del tango el compás.*
>
> *En las notas de esa musiquita*
> *Hay no sé qué vaga sensación,*
> *Que el barrio parece*
> *Impregnarse todo de emoción.*
> *Y es porque son tantos los recuerdos*
> *Que a su paso despertando va,*
> *Que llena las almas*
> *Con un gran deseo de llorar.*

To the slow gait of a poor old man / Music fills the street / With a sound like broken glass / It is the street organ at dusk. / Turning the handle / a one-legged man walks along / his wooden leg / beating time to the music.
There is in that music / a strange vague feeling / an emotion / that pervades the barrio. / Because, as he passes, he awakens / So many

*memories / filling the hearts of those who hear his music with a
desire to weep.*

*('Organito de la tarde', Street organ in the evening
— Cátulo andJosé González Castillo, 1924)*

The nascent film industry was also discovering tango – its
dramatic choreography on the silent screen was accompanied
by the tango musicians in the pit. In the musical theatre of the
day, called the *sainete*, tango had won its permanent place. And
Glücksmann's work had expanded the audience for tango. But if
all of this had won tango its legitimate place in the new Argentina,
just as the communities from which it emerged had won recognition by dint of struggle and organization as citizens of the country,
the tango was changing in this new reality.

Its words were no longer mere accompaniment to the
dance, or cheerful interludes. Contursi and the outstanding
lyricists of his generation, above all Enrique Santos Discépolo
but also Celedonio Flores, Cátulo Castillo, Eduardo Arolas and
others, were creating a new poetry of urban experience, a symbolic
universe that would bind together the disparate elements of
the new city. Contursi's lyrics, to Samuel Castriota's music,
would soon be sung at the Teatro Maipo by Carlos Gardel,
who became the embodiment of tango, its first superstar and
its first martyr.

Gardel's own transformation, from the singer with the folk
duo Gardel–Razzano presenting traditional rural music and
dressed in the *gaucho* costumes of the Argentine *pampa*, to the
suave streetwise figure in suit and homburg, mirrored the metamorphosis of tango itself. And with that change came a new cast
of characters.

DRAMATIS PERSONAE

'Mi noche triste' is more than the first tango-song; it is also in many ways the sourcebook for thousands of tangos that follow. The inhabitants of the tango world were prostitutes, pimps and tricksters, and the immigrants who shared their limited space in the newly populated barrios like La Boca and Nueva Pompeya, the crowded *arrabales* of the city outskirts and the *conventillos* wedged among the old mansions in the city centre. The scenario of the tango drama was the street, the cafés, the dance halls (*academias* and cafés), and the brothels. The props were streetlamps, trams, bottles of champagne or cheap liquor, and bar stools aplenty.

The scenario and its protagonists will reappear countless times, amid the nostalgic evocations and endless expressions of regret and yearning that echo through the tango. And it will establish too the ambiguous and contradictory relationships around which the words and the music dance. This is a poetry born of a masculinity fearful of its loss, in a world where men outnumber women, yet where sexual desire and the search for love give women the power to inflict pain, albeit they too are without social or collective power.

The singer on this sad night is a man abandoned looking back to a time of happiness now lost. His weakness and confusion are the consequences of the actions of a woman who has left him, a *milonguera* who has probably been tempted, as so many are in the world of tango, by rich men who have money but few illusions, and who are willing to pay for her company (the *bacán*). Yet the picture is more complex still. In this world of immigrants and prostitutes sharing the small pool of light from the streetlamp, surrounded by shadows, all are powerless.

El conventillo luce su traje de etiqueta;
las paicas van llegando, dispuestas a mostrar
que hay pilchas domingueras, que hay porte y hay silueta,

a los garabos reos deseosos de tanguear.
La orquesta mistonguera musita un tango fulo,
los reos se desgranan buscando, entre el montón,
la princesita rosa de ensortijado rulo
que espera a su Romeo como una bendición.

El dueño de la casa
atiende a las visitas
los pibes del convento
gritan en derredor
jugando a la rayuela,
al salto, a las bolitas,
mientras un gringo curda
maldice al Redentor.

El fuelle melodioso termina un tango papa.
Una pebeta hermosa saca del corazón
un ramo de violetas, que pone en la solapa
del garabito guapo, dueño de su ilusión.
Termina la milonga. Las minas retrecheras
salen con sus bacanes, henchidas de emoción,
llevando de esperanzas un cielo en sus ojeras
y un mundo de cariño dentro del corazón.

The slum is in its Sunday best / the girls arrive all ready to show off
/ Their best clothes, their figure and their style / and the lads all
ready to dance a tango / The dance band plays a simple tango /
the lads rush to find among the crowd / the pink princess with curls
in her hair / waiting to be blessed by her Romeo.
The owner of the house / attends to his visitors / the kids from the
slum / Rush about shouting / playing hopscotch / jumping, rolling
marbles / While a drunken foreigner / berates the Redeemer.
The tuneful bandoneon ends a fine tango / a lovely girl pulls from

her breast / a bunch of violets which she pins to the lapel / of the
handsome boy who is the object of her dreams / The dance ends, the
girls / leave with their rich boys, swelling with emotion / their eyes
full of hope / and their hearts full of love.

('Oro muerto', Dead gold – Juan Raggi, 1926)

The innocence of the street party is as brief as the tango itself.
The girls leaving joyfully with their rich boyfriends (their *bacanes*)
may well be leaving the *conventillo* for a brothel like the one at 348
Corrientes Street, commemorated in Carlos César Lenzi's emblematic tango 'A media luz' (In the half light) of 1926. Here, in the
shadowy places of transition between the city and the barrios by the
port, men could come for tea or cocktails, comfort, a dance or sex,
in the discreet second-floor flat furnished tastefully and expensively
from Harrod's store on Florida Street. It offers discretion (there is no
concierge), comfort, drugs and love – at a price. Even here the joy is
short-lived, the ecstasy a three-minute dance, the roles played out by
each partner the aspiration of people without roots. The pining
voice that sings 'Mi noche triste' is almost certainly the pimp, the
smart *compadrito* who will have watched with satisfaction as his
woman danced and made love with others. His love was also his
hope of redemption and survival in a world with very little morality.

There are others in the theatre of tango; the Mother, remembered and evoked as a woman incapable of deceit, loyal and loving,
is located in some other, previous world, in which the order of
things was uncorrupted. The Barman who listens endlessly in
silence to drunken laments from young men for whom this is almost
always the 'last binge' before dying. There is the rival, or the Rival,
another pimp fighting for the *milonguera*, or the rich man slumming
in the barrio who tempts and tantalizes her with promises of wealth
and stability. And the Madam, herself once a dancer or a prostitute,
who now shares her wisdom with the young girls she gathers round
her at establishments like the one on Corrientes Street.

There is a supporting cast too, to watch and sometimes to sympathize, sometimes to gloat. The Friend, who is loyal and concerned, but unable to alter a destiny that he sees unfolding before him. There is the Gambler, whose most famous song is Gardel and Le Pera's 'Por una cabeza' (On the nose), the embodiment of the yearning for a quick fortune that is the key to another world. And there is the Dying Lover, the Lady of the Camelias, so familiar from late-nineteenth-century literature.

Man is the victim, though his innocence is certainly open to question. The tango interweaves all these stories, in an elegant ballet of shifting fortunes and moving powers.

Contursi certainly established an idiom, an atmosphere and a universe of feeling for tango with 'Mi noche triste'. The lament for lost love, the sense of betrayal, the impotence of the song's protagonist will endlessly recur in one form or another.

'You left me with my soul in tatters . . .', he sings. For the tango 'is the complaints book of the arrabal'.[6] Woman (with the exception of the Mother of course) is the betrayer here – the one who buys and sells love. Contursi had introduced us earlier to the cynical woman in his 'Champagne tango' (1914).

Se acabaron esas minas
Que siempre se conformaban
Con lo que el bacán les daba
Si era bacán de verdad.
Hoy sólo quieren vestidos
Y riquísimas alhajas,
Coches de capota baja
Pa' pasear por la ciudad.
Nadie quiere conventillo
Ni ser pobre costurera,
Ni tampoco andar fulera . . .
Sólo quieren aparentar

Ser amigo de fulano
Que tenga mucho vento
Que alquile departamento
Que la lleve al Pigalle.

Those girls don't exist any more / the ones that just accepted things
/ took whatever the rich man gave them / if he really was so rich. /
Now they just want dresses / and fancy jewels / convertibles to ride
in / around the city.
No one wants to live in conventillos / nor be a poor seamstress / or
be less than well dressed. / They just want to put on airs / be best
friends with so-and-so / who's got plenty of money / rents them a
flat / and takes them to the Pigalle.
('Champagne Tango – Pascual Contursi, 1914)

How very far this all seems from the world of the dance,
where the man controls, manipulates and drives his woman,
expresses his domination of her, and she twists and turns to the
touch of his hand – sensual, seductive yes, but never leading. Yet
here, in the *tango-canción*, the tango-song, the woman is cynical
and manipulative, and the man, the *compadrito*, who lived from
her earnings in the past, now presents himself as the victim.
The transgressive, amoral universe of the underworld provides
the new tango-song with its dramatis personae, but its moral
universe seems to have turned upside down. Now the tangos are
'male confessions that talk overwhelmingly about women'.[7]

As he protects himself with a facade of steps that demon-
strates perfect control [the male tanguero] contemplates his
absolute lack of control in the face of history and destiny.[8]

This is one interpretation – that tango is an expression of a general
sense of alienation and powerlessness, an echo of the marginality

of the immigrant. But there is another text at work in these sometimes melodramatic pieces. The man laments his impotence
before the wiles of women, women who, as Contursi notes,
are unwilling to accept the life of decent poverty, sacrifice and
self-abnegation that awaits them in the slums and clapboard
houses of the *conventillos* and the *arrabales*.

Their unwillingness to accept a wretched fate perhaps
reflected the atmosphere of emancipation spreading among the
middle-class women of Buenos Aires. Their attendance at the
afternoon *thés dansants* was more combative and challenging
than their thoroughly respectable equivalents in New York. It
was said that the women of Buenos Aires snorted cocaine and
drank enthusiastically with their part-time afternoon gigolos,
just as their husbands did in the evenings with the *milongueras*.
The symbolic universe of the new Argentina, with its emphasis
on family and decency, was in some sense enshrined in the
Radical Party, which increasingly came to represent these values.
Yet women seemed increasingly unwilling to passively accept
their role in this new arrangement, be they middle-class women
or the working-class girls whose route out of the barrio passed
through the dance halls and cabarets. It is a curious contradiction
that the growing number of women employed in factories,
shops and increasingly in offices expressed fewer concerns with
independence and liberation, despite the level of organization
and militancy in the working class in general.[9] For even the
anarchists saw the role of women in similar ways to social
organizations – as mothers and supporters of male activity.

Rosita Quiroga, one of the early group of women tango singers,
described the trajectory of a typical *milonguera*, responding to the
criticism implicit in so many of these early tangos.

> *Yo de mi barrio era la piba más bonita*
> *En un colegio de monjas me eduqué*

Y aunque mis viejos no tenían mucha guita
Con familias bacanas me traté.
Y por culpa de este trato abacanado,
Ser niña bien fue mi única ilusión
Y olvidando por completo mi pasado,
A un magnate le entregué mi corazón.
Por su porte y su trato distinguido,
Por las cosas que me mintió al oído,
No creí que pudiera ser malvado
Un muchacho tan correcto y educado.

Sin embargo me indujo el mal hombre,
Con promesas de darme su nombre,
A dejar mi hogar abandonado
Para ir a vivir a su lado.
Y por eso que me vida se desliza
Entre el tango y el champán del cabaret;
Mi dolor se confunde en mi risa
Porque a reír mi dolor me acostumbré.

Y si encuentro algún otario que pretenda
Por el oro mis amores conseguir,
Yo lo dejo sin un cobre pa que aprenda
Y me pague lo que aquel me hizo sufrir.
Hoy bailo el tango, soy molinera
Me llaman loca y no sé qué;
Soy flor de fango, una cualquiera,
Culpa del hombre que me engañó.
Y entre las luces de mil colores
Y la alegría del cabaret,
Vendo caricias y vendo amores
Para olvidar a aquel que se fue.

I was the prettiest girl in my district / I went to a convent school /
And though my parents didn't have much money / I spent time with
rich families. / And because of that contact with wealthy people /
all I wanted was to be well off / and forgetting my past completely /
I gave my heart to a wealthy magnate. / His manner and the way he
treated me / and the lies he whispered in my ear / Made me think he
could do nothing wrong / he was too well brought up.
Yet that bad man / promised to give me his name / persuaded me to
abandon my home / and live with him. That's why now I live my life
/ between the tango and champagne cabaret / my pain flows into
my laughter / and I've got used to laughing off the pain.
And if I ever meet a man / who tries to win my heart with gold /
I'll leave him without a penny to his name to teach him a lesson /
and to get back at him for what the other put me through. I dance the
tango now, I am a cancan girl / they call me crazy and other things;
/ I come from the lower depths, / just another victim of the man
who took her for a ride. And among the coloured lights / and the joy
of the cabaret, / I sell my kisses and I sell my love / to forget the man
who left me.

> *(De mi barrio, In my district – Roberto Goyheneche, 1920–25)*

Enter the *Milonguita*, herself a victim of the men who have
abused her, on whom she takes her revenge. The tango lyricists
warn her that all pleasure is fleeting, and that this dissolute
public life will soon end when youth and beauty fade. But there
is no road back from the life she has chosen, or the carpe diem
it implies – living for the day like 'La Mina del Ford' – the girl
in the Ford.

The man who suffers an unrequited love for this fallen girl, so
easily seduced by wealth and glamour, is for the most part alone
and abandoned, suffering in eloquent images the consequences of
his loyalty and authentic love. Yet surely this is the same *compadrito*
who just shortly before had boasted of his prowess with the knife

and his ability to cheat and con vulnerable visitors to the lower
depths. His background, as we have seen, was rural in most
cases. He too was an immigrant, an exile from the changing countryside cast into the world of the *arrabal*, where survival was a
matter of skill and ruthlessness. The arts he learned transformed
him into a pimp – isolated, individualistic, using his women to
feather his own nest. He never worked, yet found the resources
to dress in self-conscious imitation of the upper classes.

His life changed as the city changed, and now the poor room
in which Contursi places him is probably in one of the working-
class neighbourhoods that have recently arisen. Perhaps he, like
the *Milonguita*, had moved out of the dockland barrio in search
of better things. His failure, as it is painted here, however, is not a
financial one but a kind of moral fall replayed against the gaudy
background of the demi-monde. All that is left to him now is
nostalgia for that world, now lost, and loquacious self-pity poured
into song.

> *Eche amigo, nomás, écheme y llene*
> *hasta el borde la copa de champán,*
> *que esta noche de farra y de alegría*
> *el dolor que hay en mi alma quiero ahogar.*
> *Es la última farra de mi vida,*
> *de mi vida, muchachos, que se va . . .*
> *mejor dicho, se ha ido tras de aquella*
> *que no supo mi amor nunca apreciar.*
>
> *Yo la quise, muchachos, y la quiero*
> *y jamás yo la podré olvidar;*
> *yo me emborracho por ella*
> *y ella quién sabe qué hará.*
> *Eche, mozo, más champán,*
> *que todo mi dolor,*

bebiendo lo he de ahogar;
y si la ven,
muchachos, díganle
que ha sido por su amor
que mi vida ya se fue.

Y brindemos, nomás, la última copa
que tal vez también ella ahora estará
ofreciendo en algún brindis su boca
y otra boca feliz la besará.
Eche, amigo, nomás, écheme y llene
hasta el borde la copa de champán,
que mi vida se ha ido tras de aquella
que no supo mi amor nunca apreciar.

Come on, my friend, fill it up / fill my glass of champagne to the
brim / on this night of booze and joy / I'm going to drown the pain
that's in my heart. / It's the last binge I'll ever have / my life is fading
away, lads . . . / or rather it's gone away with her / the woman who
never appreciated the love I had to give.
I loved her, lads, and I still do / and I'll never forget her . . . / I'm
drinking because of her. / Who knows what she's doing now. / More
champagne, barman, / I've so much pain to drink away / And if you
see her, friends / tell her / that my life drained away because of her.
So let's raise a final glass. / Perhaps she's raising her glass at this
very moment / and offering up her lips / for other fevered lips to kiss.
/ Come on, barman, more champagne / fill my champagne glass to
the brim / my life has gone, she has gone / the woman who never
understood my love.

('La última copa', The final glass – J. A Caruso, 1926)

Men are the bearers of this vision of authentic love, the seekers
after romance, the worshippers of passion. Women are more

cynical, more pragmatic, unimpressed by these promises of eternal love unless it is accompanied by material improvement.

The reality, of course, is that in this world of prostitution the women were the breadwinners, maintaining their pimps and protectors in the style to which they quickly became accustomed. For the tangos make it clear that the men never worked – it is rare for any wage-earning activity to be mentioned in tango lyrics.

The protagonists of the new tango lyrics seem strangely familiar from the fin de siècle literature of Paris. They carry echoes of Murger's *Vie de bohème* and mirror Hoffman's aimless flaneur, adrift in a city that is hostile and strange.[10] And although the language of this new poetry is the argot of the port, *lunfardo*, its imagery owes more to the late romantic Modernista movement of the turn of the century in Latin America, which borrowed heavily from Parnasse and the literary movements of Paris. Mimi reincarnated in the avenues of Buenos Aires.

Mi adorado París
no te puedo olvidar
porque yo allí
aprendí a amar.
Juventud
Que dorada pasó
Entre risas y champán
Y besos de mujer.

Oh, París, ciudad luz
y ciudad del querer
no podré olvidar
Montmartre de placer.
En ti siempre estarán
la dulce Midinette,

brindando con su amor
un verso de Musset.

¡Oh, París! ¡Oh, París de mi ensueño!
¡Oh, París! ¡Oh, París de mi amor!

My beloved Paris / I can't forget you / because it was there / that I
learned to love. / My lovely golden youth / has passed / amid
laughter and champagne / and the kisses of women.
Oh, Paris, city of light / city of love / I cannot forget / Montmartre
the place of pleasure / There will always be the sweet / Midinette /
celebrating with her love / a poem by Musset.
Oh, Paris, Paris of my dreams / Paris, Paris of my love.

('Oh, Paris' – J. A Caruso, 1924)

There is one more female presence in this world of disappointed
men and cynical women: the Mother, the exemplar of idealized
Woman, locked in the family (literally, since she never appears
outside the home), selfless and dispensing a love that requires no
recompense or even recognition; someone who is caring and
protective.

Pobre viejecita, que llorando está
por la mala hija que no volverá! . . .
Huyó de su lado tras un falso amor
y hoy la pobre madre muere de dolor . . .
Viejecita buena, deja de llorar;
que la que se ha ido ha de retornar . . .
Por la misma puerta por donde salió
ha de entrar un día a pedirte perdón.

Añora esos días de felicidad,
muy cerca de aquella que nunca vendrá;

cuando la besaba con todo su amor
y la acariciaba con loco fervor.
Y los días pasados en el dulce hogar
junto a la que un día la pudo dejar
sin ver de que al irse tras de aquel querer
destrozó la vida a quien le dio el ser.

Y una triste tarde, muy cansada ya
de esperar en vano la que no vendrá,
cerró aquellos ojos, dejó de llorar,
y al cielo la pobre se fue a descansar . . .
Y la santa madre, que tanto esperó
la vuelta de aquella que nunca volvió,
en su pobre lecho, antes de morir,
a tan mala hija supo bendecir.

Poor little old lady, who is crying / over the bad daughter who will
never come back / She fled from her side, pursuing a false love / and
today her poor mother is dying of sorrow / Stop crying, old lady /
the girl who left will return / through the same door she left by /
she'll walk in to ask your forgiveness.
She misses those happy times / beside the girl who will never come
back / she kissed her then with all her love / and caressed her with
passion / and those days at home in the distant past / with the girl
who left her / without seeing that following her love / destroyed the
life of the one who brought her into this world.
And one sad evening, weary / of waiting in vain / she closed her
eyes and ceased to weep / and took her rest in heaven. / And the
saintly mother / who waited so long / for her to return, though she
never did / in her simple bed, just before dying / gave a blessing to
her errant child.

('No llore viejecita', Don't cry little old lady – Julio Aparicio, 1930)

By 1920, tango has changed once more. The dance bands, the *orquestas tipicas*, were giving way to more sophisticated ensembles whose members were more likely now to have a musical education and be able to read music, unlike their predecessors who had tended to whistle or sing their songs to others who could note them down on paper. The ensemble allowed individuals some space for solo performance too – the tango virtuoso was emerging, like Homero Manzi and Francisco Canaro on the bandoneon or Juan D'Arienzo on piano. The orchestras were becoming larger, often including three or four bandoneons, and their tuxedos suggested sophistication rather than identification with the life of ordinary people. Dance, too, was giving way to song, as the heroes of a new age, the *Guardia Nueva* or 'New Guard', took the baton from the *Vieja Guardia* who had set tango successfully on its way. And it would be two great names – one a composer, the other an adored star of the cinema screen – who would launch tango into its new life.

5 GARDEL AND THE GOLDEN AGE

THE BOY FROM THE ABASTO

Superstars rarely come ready made, not even Carlos Gardel, the iconic figure of tango legend whose name still resonates across the Spanish-speaking world even though he died in an air crash in Colombia in 1935. For the wider world, it was Rudolph Valentino who embodied the excitement, the danger and the sexual frisson of the age of Tangomania. He always referred his viewer back to the origins of tango in the dark streets of port cities, or the shabby bars, where sailors met their prostitutes and wrestled with their pimps. Valentino personified that time of transition; he was a dancer whose body language was all that mattered, even as the silent films that made him famous moved into sound.

Tango as song and as poetry, tango as a personal drama shared the same setting, but its relationship with that background was profoundly different. With Valentino it was a theatrical backdrop and little more. But Carlos Gardel reaffirmed at every turn his re-lationship with the real world of the barrio with a sympathy and pride reflected in his mellifluous baritone voice and his gentle smile. His voice carried the early days of Argentine cinema, but his appeal went far beyond Argentina, to Venezuela and Colombia, to Cuba and to Spain, where his iconic status was elaborately constructed by a North American film industry anxious to penetrate the lucrative and growing market south of its border.

Like Argentina, Mexico had its golden age of cinema too, with music playing a central part; its singing stars, like Maria Félix and

Pedro Infante, reached a semi-divine status. The films of 'El Indio' Fernández and other key directors of the cinema of the era were set against rural backgrounds, usually during the Mexican Revolution of 1910–17. Their central characters wore the stylized clothes of the Mexican horseman (the *charro*), and sang the ballads of the border country, the *rancheras*. This imagined world of wicked landowners, downtrodden peasants and heroic strangers with beautiful singing voices reinforced a national identity in construction whose central motif was the epic story of a revolution fictionalized in film and song.[1]

Gardel was equally the focus of a nascent national symbolism, but one that lacked the heroes or victors of Mexican film. Argentine society in the late Teens and early Twenties of the century had severed its historical and cultural connections with the patrician families of historical myth – the Mitres, the Newberys, the Güiraldes and the rest. They remained powerful economic actors, of course, and continued to live out their European culture in their mansions in Belgrano, shopped at the Harrod's store on the Calle Florida and, like Jorge Luis Borges, often spoke English at home. But they were no longer the point of reference for a modern nation in construction.

The election victory of the Radical Party in 1916 was the direct result of the Sáenz Peña Law four years earlier, which marked the emergence of a new nation. Both the Law and indeed the Radical Party itself were a response to the social transformations of the preceding decades and the social weight of a population well represented by a capital city in which 50 per cent of the population had been born outside the country. Yet if the experiment in consensus and national unity, led from the now uncontested federal capital, was to be successful, a new imaginary would need to emerge which could embrace and unify these disparate communities. It would also have to convince a working-class population deeply suspicious of a system of parliamentary

Carlos Gardel.

democracy in which it had no voice and was dominated by ideas that reinforced that distance. And that would require a language of nationhood rooted in its shared experience, its specific icons and its distinctive voice. It found all these in Carlos Gardel.

Gardel was probably born in Toulouse on 11 December 1890; he moved to Argentina with his mother when he was six. His street friends in the Abasto district where he grew up called him 'Frenchie'; they were immigrants too and their playground was the street, where Carlos and the others were regularly picked up for petty misdemeanours. As a teenager, he frequented the city's theatres, where in this first decade he would have seen and heard singers in the Spanish light operas called *zarzuelas*, as well as visiting grand opera companies from Italy and France. The music of the

Argentine countryside, the often improvised ballads sung to a guitar accompaniment, were popular in the *arrabales*, where the recent migrants to the city gathered to sing and listen. This much is known; most of the rest is legend or gossip. Gardel's origins have moved around continuously and his fairly ordinary working-class past transmuted into youthful brushes with the criminal classes, an early career as a gigolo, and the status of the bastard child of the aristocracy. Gardel himself made no great effort to set the record straight; the enigmas and the mysteries, after all, sustained the myth.

The popular *música criolla*, the Argentine folk music tradition now largely written and formalized rather than the history of improvisation from which it came, won Gardel's interest and attention, and in 1911 he began to work with José Razzano in an increasingly popular singing duo. They would continue to perform together for more than a decade, making their first recordings in 1913. One night they were invited to a post-theatre performance at the exclusive and luxurious Armenonville Club, where they were cheered to the rooftops and offered a more permanent contract, prompting Gardel to say, as legend has it, 'My God, for that much money I'd wash the dishes as well as sing'.[2]

Gardel and Razzano were well known in the theatres of Buenos Aires. The duo lasted until 1925, but Gardel had already moved long before that into singing tango. His recording of 'Mi noche triste' in 1917 was a huge and instant success – it sold 100,000 copies. He had first sung it in Montevideo, after its composer Pascual Contursi approached Gardel at a concert. Razzano was sceptical in the beginning, but Gardel began increasingly to perform tangos, and by 1920 he and Razzano had more or less abandoned their old repertoire in favour of this immensely popular new form.

This was also the beginning of the age of radio. His partner's recurring throat problems left Gardel to take centre stage, which he did not just in Argentina. His recordings were popular in Spain in particular, and in the early Twenties he made a series of tours there. He was prolific; in a relatively short career he recorded over 500 tangos, many of them his own compositions with lyrics by his constant collaborator, the journalist Alfredo Le Pera. But these came later. More importantly, he was the interpreter and performer of the iconic tangos of Contursi, Celedonio Flores and others. Gardel was the voice of the Golden Age of Tango.

The *Guardia Nueva* had taken tango from the dance floor to the stage, the theatre and the cabaret circuit, with Gardel at its head. Musically, it was perhaps a more adventurous time, as the opportunities for solo performance multiplied in this new context. Tango was certainly becoming smoother, more sophisticated, less tied to the rhythm of dance. Its dramatic narrative became increasingly important and the bandoneon not simply its background, but a companion to the words, almost a commentator on the relationship between the past and the present of tango.

The bandoneon is impossible to play without involvement; it engages the whole body, and not just the fingers and the arms. The drama of the song is somehow enacted, and the singer and the player exchange regular glances of complicity.

THE BANDONEON PLAYER: GERARDO'S STORY

I'm a student of the bandoneon and I respect the history of the instrument. It's a diatonic aerophone, that is, it has a different range opening and closing. The arrangement of buttons is quite illogical because instead of notes being next to one another, they're all over the place. There are half a dozen buttons at each side that give you a chord opening and a fifth closing. That was logical when it was invented in Germany with a harmonic relationship between them. But when it arrived in Argentina, musicians kept asking for notes to be added, so they were apparently randomly added around those central buttons. But it's only apparently illogical because having two notes next to each other an octave apart probably makes it easier to play a tango. And some people say that because of that arrangement, it's the only keyboard for playing tango.

The tango is its own music, even though it is related to classical music and Argentine folk music too. It has harmonics, cadences, passages between the bass notes, so the structure of tango music is binary, verse and choruses repeated twice, though sometimes it has three parts. The harmonic richness is huge. That happened when tango musicians began to study music because the first generation played by ear. The early bandoneon players didn't know the instruments and didn't read music so they learned by ear. That was the Guardia Vieja.

They played in the brothels. That's a good story because the bandoneon was invented in Germany to be played in churches instead of the harmonium. But it never really became popular there and ended up in the brothels of Buenos Aires. When it arrived, tangos were played on guitars and flutes and later the piano. By 1900, the bandoneon was the dominant instrument in tango. Then around 1915 came the Guardia Nueva with De Caro and Arolas, a phenomenal composer.

The bandoneon has its own vocabulary and it would be good for someone to collect all those terms that musicians used. 'La mugre', for example (literally, 'the muck') – musicians would say 'put in some muck' and you know it means adding a semitone above or below the main note. Of course, that doesn't appear in the written score and if musicians come from other traditions, they play what they read and it isn't tango. There's a big difference between the way it's written and the way it's played. And I think that's closely linked to the singer. If you want to learn how to phrase tango, you have to listen to the singers. It's like the way the bagpipes are played in the north of Scotland – they follow the singers.

A tango musician will add to the phrasing. And before the Golden Age of tango, the orchestras were working orchestras – they had to compose and arrange their own music. That's the origin of the 'yeites', the way in which the player moves chromatically between one note and another instead of going directly. They're dramatic runs, I suppose. Rock musicians still use the term in Argentina – though the word comes from tango.

It isn't the same as jazz because tango musicians tended not to improvise. The music was written and the musicians had to stick to the composition and the arrangement. These orchestras were playing for dance. Aníbal Troilo, for example, composed some wonderful pieces and there was no one to equal his bandoneon playing. But he was a working musician and he didn't stray from the music. Troilo felt his music, he spoke as he wrote and he had tango in his soul. You can see on the videos that he had a connection with the instrument. I play other instruments and all the people I know who have taken up bandoneon after playing another instrument agree that the relationship you have with the bandoneon is completely different from any other instrument. He was very professional and when Astor Piazzola worked with him, he said, 'Look don't decorate, just play the music.'

Your relationship with your instrument is physical. Your fingers don't produce the sound of the bandoneon; they just press buttons. The different articulations and attacks can be compared to the piano. It has a shorter range, of course – five and a half octaves. Like the cello, you can sustain notes forever, opening and closing. But all the sound comes from moving keys, from moving the bellows – so it is very physical.

I'm a bit mystical about the bandoneon. I'm a percussionist and I have my favourite drums but I never talked to any of them. But I do talk to my bandoneon, though it doesn't usually answer.

Why did I take up bandoneon? I grew up under the last military government and tango wasn't popular. As far as young people were concerned, tango was like a closed sect. You never saw people out and about doing tango. It just wasn't cool – and it was miserable too. And yet tango was a backcloth to my growing up – I listened to it on the radio, my parents played tango in the house, and I liked it. But tango was the music of old people, and the bandoneon was a kind of secret instrument. People said you had to start learning when you were five or six. That's because tango was the rock and roll of its time and parents would buy their kids a bandoneon like today's parents will buy their kids an electric guitar.

That's why they started so young because in their day the bandoneon was music. It is very difficult – some people say it's the most difficult instrument to learn. You can't see the keyboard, so you have to learn where the notes are, and you have to learn four keyboards – right and left closing and opening. If you make it through the first six months, that's it. You're in love. Lots of people give up. But I started late and I took it up knowing I wouldn't ever tame it – and I know I never will dominate it. Because the bandoneon has a memory, music inside, tastes and smells. I don't know the history of my instrument, but I know it has a history of its own. It's had two previous owners, it has seen the world. The bandoneon has its secrets and it will never give them up. You have to draw them out, playing, practising. And if someone else plays my instrument, it will sound completely different. It is so personal that everything you do influences the sound. I've never felt such frustration, such ecstasy, such love.

The tone of the tango-song of the 1920s is nostalgic, plangent (just like the bandoneon), evoking a lost world within living memory. For the most part, the story is told from the margins of the barrio, its voice predominantly male and complaining of betrayal and misunderstanding, of lost love and despair. Its moral universe is conservative and masculine. The likely history of its implied narrator – obviously a recently retired *compadrito* – the romantic story of love and devotion misunderstood and rejected cannot hide the fact that it was the woman who was the breadwinner and he its beneficiary. The setting for this drama is urban; the light cast by the yellow street lights over the singer waiting, hopelessly, for his ex-lover to pass by, though she has deserted him for a rich man who will keep her, as long as she is young and beautiful. And when it becomes clear that he can never win her back, then all that remains is the long slide into oblivion recounted in one of Gardel's most popular tangos 'Cuesta abajo' (Downhill).

> *Era, para mí, la vida entera,*
> *como un sol de primavera,*
> *mi esperanza y mi pasión.*
> *Sabía que en el mundo no cabía*
> *toda la humilde alegría*
> *de mi pobre corazón.*
> *Ahora, cuesta abajo en mi rodada,*
> *las ilusiones pasadas*
> *yo no las puedo arrancar.*
> *Sueño con el pasado que añoro,*
> *el tiempo viejo que lloro*
> *y que nunca volverá.*
>
> *Por seguir tras de su huella*
> *yo bebí incansablemente*
> *en mi copa de dolor,*

pero nadie comprendía
que, si todo yo lo daba
en cada vuelta dejaba
pedazos de corazón.
Ahora, triste, en la pendiente,
solitario y ya vencido
yo me quiero confesar:
si aquella boca mentía
el amor que me ofrecía,
por aquellos ojos brujos
yo habría dado siempre más.

She was my whole life / Like spring sunshine / My hope and my
passion. / She knew that the world wasn't big enough / For the
humble joy I felt / In my heart. / Now, sliding downhill / I can't get
rid of / Those illusions of the past / that past / I dream of, long for
/ The old times I weep for / That will never return.
Because I followed her trail / I drank relentlessly / From my glass of
pain / But no-one understood / That if I gave everything / I left
pieces of myself behind / At every turn. / Now, sad and in decline /
Alone and defeated / I want to confess. / If that mouth lied /
When it offered me love / I would have given anything / For those
bewitching eyes.

('Cuesta abajo', Downhill – Alfredo Le Pera, 1934)

But beauty fades and fate brings the arrogant mistress back
to the reality of ageing and poverty. It is as if the man who sings
is claiming for himself a kind of moral superiority, though he
too has been the victim of passions and blind desire that led
him in so many tangos to leave behind the lodestar of a moral
life – the mother who is home, stability and selfless love. Many
tangos evoke the place of innocence, of childhood, its location
indeterminate but its role in the drama clear. It is the time

before corruption, a rural Eden overseen by a caring, undemand-
ing mother who seems to be in an endless posture of waiting
for the son or daughter to acknowledge the error of their
ways and return, laden with guilt, to 'la casita de mis viejos',
to quote a famous tango by Juan Carlos Cobián, 'the home of
my parents'. The 'sienes plateadas', the silver temples, are a
conceit repeated in many tangos, to mark both the passing of
time and the burden of experience; only the ailing mother can
offer absolution, in the absence of any religious personnel, and
the unconditional love whose absence in the urban underworld
is so often recalled.

Carlos Gardel, however, largely because of the flawless
beauty of his voice, lifted tango from its dangerous closeness
to sentimentality and invested words and music with a passionate intensity. Gardel was more than simply a singer, the *zorzal*,
or thrush, he was named after; he was also *el morocho del Abasto*,
'the dark-skinned boy from the Abasto district', the embodiment
of the tango story. All these things prepared the ground for
superstardom of a new kind – in and beyond Argentina, and in
the new medium of film.

There is a suggestion that he was first approached by Paramount during a hugely successful tour in Paris in 1928–9 (70,000
records were sold in three months while he was there).[3] His first
appearance on celluloid (other than bit parts in two much earlier
silent films) was in late 1930, in ten short films of his best-known
tangos filmed in Paris and directed by Eduardo Morera. Paramount did eventually get their man a year later, when he filmed
Luces de Buenos Aires (*Lights of Buenos Aires*), directed by Adelqui
Millar, which included his famous line 'Tomo y obligo' ('I drink
and I buy rounds'). Paramount was desperately seeking to enter
the Latin American market, and in 1932 contracted Gardel for
three more films, to be directed by Louis Garnier. It was Garnier
who introduced Gardel to Alfredo Le Pera in Paris in 1932 (though

they had met briefly before) and set in motion the intensely creative
but short-lived collaboration between the singer and the lyricist.
Le Pera was a journalist and theatre critic who was employed by
Paramount to write the scripts for Gardel's films and the lyrics of
the songs they included. In 1934, produced by Western Electric
and distributed by Paramount, Gardel made three more films, all
filmed in New York: *Cuesta abajo* (*Downhill*), *El tango en Broadway*
and *El día que me quieras* (*The day you love me*), which included two
of Gardel's most loved (and most beautifully written) tangos – 'El
día que me quieras' and the glorious 'Volver'. Le Pera's contribution
to Gardel's career, and his posthumous fame, is not often recognized. But Le Pera's brief was to write for Gardel in a language
that would resonate throughout Latin America, and tell a story
that was universal. For Paramount, Gardel was the centre of its
planned conquest of the Latin American market. Indeed, their
ambitions were grander still, for they envisaged a future for him
as an English-language star (one of the passengers killed with him
in the crash that ended his life was José Playa, his English tutor).
Unfortunately, Gardel's command of English proved disappoint-
ingly tenuous. Instead he embarked on a tour of a Latin America,
where he played everywhere to adoring crowds. His brief visit
to Venezuela is commemorated in a popular and frequently
performed play *El día que me quieras* by José Ignacio Cabrujas,
in which his arrival provokes a crisis between the members of
a bourgeois family. Elvira, the jilted spinster daughter, reports
excitedly on Gardel's arrival in Caracas.

> Did you see the flags? . . . There isn't a flower to be had in the
> whole city. If you got ill and wanted a flower before you died
> you wouldn't find one anywhere. Tonight the Principal Theatre
> smells of magnolia. He was all dressed in black. Did you hear?
> . . . And not a drop of sweat on his whole body. Not even
> when he was feeding the pigeons in the square. Not a bead of

perspiration on his forehead, and everyone's saying – look he
doesn't sweat, Gardel doesn't sweat . . .[4]

Gardel and Le Pera flew on to Medellín in Colombia, where a
runway crash prematurely ended the life of them both.

Gardel's funeral procession to La Chacarita cemetery in Buenos
Aires in March 1935 was the largest public gathering ever seen in the
city. He was mourned, and continues to be mourned in Medellín
and across the continent. He was in every sense a superstar.

But what was it in the music that created such admiration
within Argentina and Latin America and across the world? This
was a very different tango fever from the craze that hit Europe
and the u.s. immediately before the First World War. At that time,
the exoticism and overt sensuality of the dance, its identification
with a dangerous world of the shadows, where criminality,
prostitution and transgression prevailed, was what drew a new
generation towards tango. Perhaps its riskiness, its moral ambiguity
reflected a world on edge, full of portents of disaster and the
winds of change – what George Dangerfield had described for
Britain in *The Strange Death of Liberal England*.[5] Gardel's songs were
framed by a very different worldview, one that closely reflected
the changed perspectives of postwar tango in Argentina, and
which was then refined and honed for a cosmopolitan audience
growing used to cinema musicals and the high production values
of Hollywood in the early Thirties.

What were the elements of the tangos that Gardel sang?
Musically, they were rich and complex; their lush orchestration and
sophisticated presentation were matched by the quality of both
poetry and voice. Gardel presented himself to the world not as a
disappointed pimp abandoned by his ambitious protégée, but rather
as a much more recognizable romantic hero. The lyrics were poetic,
and had for the most part abandoned the *lunfardo* that still tied the
tangos of, for example, Celedonio Flores, to its history. And although

Gardel recorded a huge proportion of the tango repertoire, including the work of Flores and the great Enrique Santos Discépolo (to whom we will come in a moment), the tangos that he sang on screen and for which he is widely remembered were essentially romantic ballads. They shared the nostalgia, the longing for a lost and idealized past, the preoccupation with loyal and devoted men abandoned by women whose shallow self-interest had deposited them in the arms of wealthy but worthless protectors. But they relocated those feelings in a less specific world and universalized them. One of Gardel's most famous songs, 'Silencio en la noche', transfers some of tango's central themes to the fields of Flanders and a First World War in which Argentina played no part.

> Silencio en la noche.
> Ya todo está en calma.
> El músculo duerme,
> la ambición trabaja.
>
> Un clarín se oye.
> Peligra la Patria.
> Y al grito de guerra
> los hombres se matan
> cubriendo de sangre
> los campos de Francia.
>
> Hoy todo ha pasado.
> Renacen las plantas.
> Un himno a la vida
> los arados cantan.
> Y la viejecita
> de canas muy blancas
> se quedó muy sola,
> con cinco medallas

que por cinco héroes
la premió la Patria.

Silence in the night / Everything is calm / the muscles at rest /
ambition at work.
A bugle sounds / the nation is in danger / and with war cries on
their lips / men kill / covering with blood / the fields of France.
Today everything has passed / the plants are reborn / the ploughs
sing / a hymn to life. / And the little old lady / her hair a pure white
/ sits very much alone / with five medals / which the Nation
awarded her / for the five heroes she bore.
  ('Silencio en la noche', Silence in the night – Gardel / Le Pera, 1932)

The most famous of all their collaborations, however, is a sort
of resumé of the tango story. 'Volver' is lyrically and musically
moving and beautiful – but it takes tango into a different moral
universe where there is little in the way of danger.[6]

Yo adivino el parpadeo
de las luces que a lo lejos,
van marcando mi retorno.
Son las mismas que alumbraron,
con sus pálidos reflejos,
hondas horas de dolor.
Y aunque no quise el regreso,
siempre se vuelve al primer amor.
La quieta calle donde el eco dijo:
'Tuya es su vida, tuyo es su querer',
bajo el burlón mirar de las estrellas
que con indiferencia hoy me ven volver.

Volver,
con la frente marchita,

las nieves del tiempo
platearon mi sien.
Sentir, que es un soplo la vida,
que veinte años no es nada,
que febril la mirada
errante en las sombras
te busca y te nombra.
Vivir,
con el alma aferrada
a un dulce recuerdo,
que lloro otra vez.

Tengo miedo del encuentro
con el pasado que vuelve
a enfrentarse con mi vida.
Tengo miedo de las noches
que, pobladas de recuerdos,
encadenan mi soñar.
Pero el viajero que huye,
tarde o temprano detiene su andar.
Y aunque el olvido que todo destruye,
haya matado mi vieja ilusión,
guarda escondida una esperanza humilde,
que es toda la fortuna de mi corazón.

I glimpse the blinking lights / in the distance / that mark my
return. / They are the same ones / whose pale reflections / shed
their light on deeper sorrows in the past. / And though I never
wanted to return / you always do come back to your first love. /
The quiet street whose echo tells you: / 'This was your life, these
were your loves', / under the mocking gaze of the stars / that
watch me with indifference at this moment of return.
Coming back / with furrowed brow / and silver temples. /

Feeling / that life is a single breath / that twenty years pass in
a moment / that a fevered glance / wandering in the shadows/
seeks you and calls your name. / Coming back/with your soul
tied/to a sweet memory / that you weep for once again.
I'm afraid of what I'll find / in the past that's now returning / to
confront the life I've lived. / I'm afraid of the nights / that, full of
memories / will occupy my dreams. / But the traveller who tries to
flee / sooner or later must halt his steps. / And if the forgetfulness
that destroys everything / has destroyed my old illusions / it
still conceals a modest hope / that is the only fortune that
my heart retains.

('Volver', Returning – A. Le Pera, 1935)

Gardel's appearance and dress had always been emblematic of
tango's origin – the homburg, the fitted suit, the gentle and seductive
voice of an ordinary young man. There was never a sense that he
was a working person; how he earned a living was left unspecified,
like every tango protagonist. And Gardel's private life was also deliberately kept mysterious, though he always presented the minimal
attributes of the tango protagonist – a man but not a *machista*
(compare the Golden Age of Mexican cinema, for example), without
swagger but intense and passionate, a gambler (but in the more
genteel world of horse racing), a lover (but with one long-term
stable partner, Margarita).

In Argentina itself tango's transformation from the transgressive
expression of a marginal world into the emblematic expression of
a new national community – urban, cosmopolitan and modern –
accompanied Gardel's rise to fame. And his mythic status and
tragic death confirmed the register and character of the tango
through its continuing heyday until the mid-1940s.

The tango can be seen as a discourse on human suffering and
the negation of real and sincere happiness for both men and

women. Happiness seems possible only if persons are grounded in their behaviour by sincere and authentic love.[7]

The romantic is male, by and large, the women who are the object of his passionate admiration are moved by other, more pragmatic considerations – the good life, comfort, and the pursuit of a power that youthful sexuality brings.

Gardel's early death did not bring an immediate end to the Golden Age of Tango. On the contrary, his death created a highly profitable myth for the music and film industries; even after death, Gardel continued to lead the globalization of tango.

Tango was not only sung by men, however. Among the very early tango singers were women, like Azucena Maizani, who did break into this male preserve – though Maizani in those early years usually appeared in male dress. The *Guardia Nueva* and the emergence of *tango-canción* also brought to prominence a small group of women singers – Rosita Quiroga and the brash Uruguayan Tita Merello among them. Talking pictures introduced a new generation of female stars, like Libertad Lamarque and Mercedes Simone, who would take their place among the pantheon of tango greats. Yet the characters they portrayed in their music were very rarely different from the women implied in the songs of Contursi or Celedonio Flores and of whom Gardel sang so beautifully. Rosita Quiroga's version of 'De mi barrio' is one example.

Azucena Maizani's 'Pero yo sé' might well be an answer to the accusation so often repeated by men, and shifts the responsibility and the challenging gaze back to the emptiness of the rich boy's life. She may serve him in return for reward, but she clearly understands the nature of the relationship.

Con todo tu brillo con toda tu andanza
Llevaste tu vida tan sólo al placer

Con todo el dinero que siempre has tenido
Todos tus caprichos lograste vencer
Pensar que ese brillo que fácil ostentas
No sabe la gente que es puro disfraz;
Tu orgullo de necio muy bien los engaña
No quieres que nadie lo sepa jamás.

Pero yo sé
Vivís pensando un querer
Que querés hallar olvido
Cambiando tanta mujer
Yo sé que en las madrugadas
Cuando la farra dejás
Sentís tu pecho oprimido
Por un recuerdo querido
Y te pones a llorar.

With all your flashy appearance and your moves about town / your life was a pursuit of pleasure / with all the money you've always had / you could satisfy all your whims / But do you think that people don't know / that it's all just a facade / your foolish pride might fool them / you want nobody to know.
But I know / that you're yearning for love / that you're looking to forget / by moving from woman to woman / I know that when the dawn comes / when the party's over for the night / you feel the weight on your chest / of a much loved memory / and you begin to weep.
('Pero yo sé', But I know – Azucena Maizani, 1928)

AFTER GARDEL

The *Guardia Vieja* orchestras of Francisco Canaro, Juan de Dios Filiberto, Roberto Firpo and others still played for dancing; their vocalists would sing choruses or interludes. The *Guardia Nueva*, by contrast – Julio de Caro, Osvaldo Pugliese, Pedro Maffia – increasingly played to audiences who listened to them and their singers. After Gardel's death, a new generation of fine dramatic singers emerged in his wake and in his honour – Roberto Goyeneche, Francisco Fiorentino (who sang with Troilo), Susana Rinaldi and others.

Tango-canción was becoming a national music, an acoustic emblem of the new Argentina. Its references to a rural world belonged to the collective past; the present was resolutely urban, masculine and cosmopolitan. Though the lyrics were now almost entirely in Spanish, they were coloured with scattered words in *lunfardo*, references to the barrio where tango was born. But increasingly the specific condition of the excluded immigrant labourer restricted to the city margins was translated into a different kind of statement, a comment on the human condition, a universal experience of isolation and regret rediscovered in a local setting. That is what the classics like 'Volver' illustrate.

DISCÉPOLO

> That discontent, that ill humor, that vague bitterness, that undefined and latent anger against everything and against every-one which is almost the quintessence of the average Argentine.[8]

Of all tango lyricists and composers, the words and music of Enrique Santos Discépolo have survived the many metamorphoses that tango song has undergone. 'Yira Yira' (On and On), 'Cambalache' (The Junk Shop) and 'Qué Vachaché' (Who Cares?) define the melancholy mood of tango. More than that, his work is imbued with a vision of the world and the people in it, which in some sense encapsulates the history of tango, of Buenos Aires as well as the existential crises of modern urban man. Tango has not so much abandoned its origins as given them new expression in more global, more timeless terms. Carlos Gardel sang everything that Discépolo wrote – but he did more than simply sing. He expressed in words and music the sense of abandon and isolation that many of Discépolo's best known tangos describe. While much of Gardel's music, particularly his film performances, is sustained by lush orchestration and lengthy musical introductions, he sings 'Cambalache' to the accompaniment of a single guitar, its unadorned form a reinforcement of its symbolic universe.

Que el mundo es y será una porquería
Ya lo sé;
En el quinientos seis
Y en el dos mil también.
Que siempre ha habido chorros,
Maquiavelos y estafaos,
Contentos y amargados
Valores y dublés,
Pero que el siglo veinte es un despliegue
De maldad insolente
Y no hay quien lo niegue;
Vivimos revolcaos en un merengue
Y en un mismo lodo todos manoseaos.

Hoy resulta que es lo mismo
Ser derecho que traidor,
Ignorante, sabio, chorro,
Generoso estafador.
Todo es igual; nada es mejor;
Lo mismo un burro que un gran profesor . . .

Siglo veinte, cambalache,
El que no llora no mama
Y el que no afana es un gil.

Dale nomás, dale que va,
Que allá en el horno nos vamos a encontrar.
No pienses más, échate a un lao,
Que a nadie le importa que naciste honrao
Que es lo mismo el que labura
Noche y día como un buey
Que el que vive de los otros,
Que el que mata o el que cura
O está fuera de la ley.&&

The world is and always will be a junkheap / You don't have to tell
me that. / In the year 506 / Or in 2000, / it'll be the same / There
have always been thieves / Con men and victims, / Happy and bitter
people / Honest men and hypocrites. / The twentieth century's
just a stage / For insolence and evil doing / And no one can tell
me otherwise; / We're all in a mess / Rolling in the same shit.
Today no one sees any difference / Between loyalty and treachery, /
Ignorance, wisdom, robbery / Or generous trickery. / It's all the
same; nothing's better than anything else; / A donkey's worth the
same as a professor.
Twentieth century, junkheap, / if you don't cry you don't eat /
if you don't cheat you're a fool / A little bit here, a little bit there. /
We'll all meet in the fire down below. / Don't think about it, just
move out of the way, / Nobody gives a damn if you were born honest.
/ The man who works day and night / Like a slave is no better or
worse / Than the man who lives off others / No better the doctor
than the killer / Or the outlaw. / Twentieth century, junkheap.
('Cambalache', The Junk Shop – Discépolo, 1935)

'Cambalache' is sung defiantly, its voice angry and resentful. It
does not speak of resistance so much as protest – the lonely
protest of the individuals who tried to find their way out of the
city margins but were defeated.

The first of Discépolo's tangos to be performed, 'Qué Vachaché', was presented to an extremely unappreciative public in Montevideo, Uruguay, in 1926. It was booed off stage. Perhaps it was the nihilism, the despair of its most famous lines (echoed later in 'Cambalache') that offended the public at the Teatro Nacional. Or perhaps its mood was just a little ahead of its time, two years too early for the Great Crash, the crisis in the u.s. economy in 1929 that would spread chaos and collapse across the world.

¿Te crees que al mundo lo vas a arreglar vos?
Si aquí ni Dios rescata lo perdido . . .
Lo que hace falta es empacar mucha moneda
Vender el alma, rifar el corazón,
Tirar la poca decencia que te queda . . .
Plata, plata, plata . . . plata otra vez . . .
Así es posible que morfes todos los días,
Tengas amigos, casa, nombre . . . y lo que quieras vos.
El verdadero amor se ahogó en la sopa;
La panza es reina y el dinero Dios.

D'you think you can set the world to rights? / Not even God can retrieve the situation . . . / What you need to do is carry lots of cash / sell your soul, raffle off your heart / Get rid of the little bit of decency you've still got left / Money, money, money . . . and money once again. / That's how you'll be sure of eating every day / of having friends, a home, a reputation . . . whatever. / Real love just drowned in the soup / The belly's queen and money's God.
('Que vachaché', What the hell – Enrique Santos Discépolo, 1929)

Yet Discépolo's 'Esta noche me emborracho' (Tonight I'm getting drunk), written in the same year, explored a more recognizable theme of the deserted man drinking away his sorrows and bemoaning his woman's disloyalty, and won instant popularity.

In 1930, the much loved Uruguayan singer, Tita Merello, recorded 'Que vachaché'; this time it was very differently and enthusiastically received. The times, after all, had changed.

Discépolo's writing held to the language of the street, a counterpoint to the more neutral romantic balladry that cinema was encouraging. Gardel bridged both idioms, both worldviews. In Discépolo, that melancholy individualism became a model of man abandoned in the world, alone in the universe. Significantly, it *was* always man – the experience of women was not approached in the same way in the tango. In some senses, it was the weakness or vulnerability of women that was emphasized; men, by contrast, could aspire to the noble failure of Greek heroes. But Discépolo's work was not simply an existential statement. It was also, albeit indirectly, a comment on the specific social reality of the early 1930s in Argentina. Rather as Busby Berkeley's glorious musicals both belied and distracted from the realities of the Great Depression (it was a very long distance from '42nd Street' to 'The Grapes of Wrath'), Gardel expressed a painful experience in an idiom, musical and linguistic, that somehow consoled and reassured his audience.

Yet tango did also offer some direct critical comment on that reality, spoken in the voice of ordinary people. Enrique Cadícamo, another great lyricist of the Golden Age, lamented 'Al mundo le falta un tornillo' (The world's got a screw loose).

> Todo el mundo está en la estufa,
> Triste, amargado, sin garufa,
> Neurasténico y cortao . . .
> Se acabaron los robustos . . .
> Si hasta yo que daba gusto
> ¡Cuatro kilos he bajado!
>
> Hoy no hay guita si de asalto
> Y el puchero está tan alto

Que hay que usar un trampolín.
Si habrá crisis, bronca y hambre
Que el que compra un poco de fiambre
Hoy se morfa hasta el piolín . . .

Y el honrao se ha vuelto chorro
Porque en su fiebre de ahorro
El se 'afana' por guarder . . .
Al mundo le falta un tornillo,
¡qué venga un mecánico!
Pa'ver si lo puede arreglar.

Everyone's complaining/sad, bitter, with nothing to celebrate /
neurotic and short of cash / . . . No more big men around / Look
at me, I used to look good / But I've lost four kilos.
There's no money around, you can't even steal it / The saucepan's so
high up / You need a trampoline to reach it / There must be a crisis,
hunger, anger / When the one who can afford a bit of meat / has to
feed everyone on the street . . .
And the honest man has turned to stealing. / He tries so hard to save
/ That he steals from other people . . . / Just to have something to
save / The world's got a screw loose / Where's there a mechanic /
Who can put all this to rights?

('*Al mundo le falta un tornillo*', The world's got a screw loose
– Enrique Cadícamo, 1933)

By 1930, the radical (or Radical) revolution that Irigoyen had
promised was in tatters. The society remained as divided as ever,
and although the working class had given him their enthusiastic
support in 1916, the limits of the compact became clear three
years later when a wave of strikes was brutally repressed in what
became known as the 'Tragic Week' of 1919. It heralded a brief
period of recession followed by a decade of relative prosperity

under the more conservative presidency of Alvear, who replaced Yrigoyen in 1922. When Yrigoyen returned to the post in 1928, the economic storm clouds were already gathering over the U.S. economy – and any crisis there would immediately affect an Argentine economy dependent on its exports to the richer markets of the north and west. The prosperity of the 1920s had certainly improved the lives of the middle classes.

> *Antes femenina era la mujer*
> *Pero con la moda se ha echado a perder,*
> *Antes no mostraba más que rostro y pie*
> *Pero hoy muestra todo lo que quieren ver*
> *Hoy todas las chicas parecen varón*
> *Fuman, toman whiskey y usan pantaloon.*

> *Women used to be feminine / But fashion has finished with all that / They used to show no more than their faces and a foot / Now they'll show you anything if you ask to look / Today the girls all look like men / They smoke, drink whiskey and wear trousers.*
> *('La mina del Ford', The Girl in the Ford – Pascual Contursi, 1924)*

Ford had in fact opened its first car plant in Buenos Aires in 1917, and General Motors followed in 1925. Car sales reached 436,000 (and 63,000 in Buenos Aires alone) by 1930.

Yet, for the majority of workers, living standards had barely risen. Even in 1937, 60 per cent of working-class families still lived in one room, as so many immigrant families had been obliged to when they arrived in this new land.[9] But only a tiny minority still lived in the *conventillos* of those times. The economic crash, however, had devastating and immediate effects. And the once popular Yrigoyen's refusing resolutely to appear in public more than was absolutely necessary, which had once created about him a certain air of mystery, now enraged the victims of economic decline.

Crowds attacked and trashed his house. And in 1930 he was overthrown by a military coup. It seems likely that, with 90,000 unemployed in the capital alone, it was Discépolo's lyrics that most closely reflected the real feelings of working people in the early 1930s. Gardel, on the other hand, provided a kind of utopian alternative, a dreamworld of handsome heroes and beautiful heroines who sang to one another and danced a tango without rage or despair.

While brothels had been suppressed in 1919, further restrictions on prostitution by the new military government after 1930 underscored its conservatism and its backward glance. The slow renewal of economic activity after 1932 occurred under conditions of repression. Tango's social comments were limited and restrained by and large – though its origins and its audience were overwhelmingly working class, their lives and experiences were only rarely reflected there. An exception was 'Lunes' (Monday):

> *Un catedrático escarba su bolsillo*
> *pa' ver si un níquel le alcanza pa' un complete . . .*
> *Ayer –¡qué dulce!–, la fija del potrillo;*
> *hoy -¡qué vinagre!-, rompiendo los boletos . . .*
> *El almanaque nos bate que es lunes,*
> *que se ha acabado la vida bacana,*
> *que viene al humo una nueva semana*
> *con su mistongo programa escorchador.*
>
> *Rumbeando pa'l taller*
> *va Josefina,*
> *que en la milonga, ayer,*
> *la iba de fina.*
> *La reina del salón*
> *ayer se oyó llamar . . .*
> *Del trono se bajó*

pa'ir a trabajar . . .
El lungo Pantaleón
ata la chata
de traje fulerón
y en alpargata.
Ayer en el Paddock
jugaba diez y diez . . .
Hoy va a cargar
carbón al Dique 3.

Piantó el domingo del placer,
bailongo, póker y champán.
Hasta el más seco pudo ser
por diez minutos un bacán.
El triste lunes se asomó,
mi sueño al diablo fue a parar,
la redoblona se cortó
y pa'l laburo hay que rumbear.

Pero, ¿qué importa que en este monte criollo
hoy muestre un lunes en puerta el almanaque?
Si en esa carta caímos en el hoyo,
ya ha de venir un domingo que nos saque.
No hay mal, muchachos, que dure cien años
y ligaremos también un bizcocho . . .
A lo mejor acertamos las ocho
¡y quién te ataja ese día, corazón! . . .

The punter scours his pocket / to see if he's got enough to place a bet
/ Yesterday was fun / the inside info on a horse / Today, how bitter!
Tearing up the tickets. / The calendar says it's Monday / that the
rich man's life is over / that it's Monday and another week begins /
with its boring routine.

On her way to work / goes Josefina / who looked so grand / at the dance yesterday. / I heard her called / the queen of the dance hall, yesterday . . . today she got down from her throne / to go to work . . . / Tall Pantaleon / half dead / in a crumpled suit / and rough shoes / yesterday in the Paddock / put on ten to win and ten to place . . . / Today he's off / to carry coal to Dock No.3.

Sunday – the day of pleasure / dancing, poker and champagne / when even someone who's skint / can play the rich man for 10 minutes. / Came sad Monday / My dreams went to the devil / the Yankee fell at the first fence / And I have to get to work.

But what does it matter that in this game / the calendar says it's Monday? / On the turn of a card it's back to the pit / until Sunday when we climb out / Nothing evil lasts a hundred years / And maybe we'll get laid / Maybe we'll win an eight-way accumulator / Maybe that's the day we make it, dear heart!

('Lunes', Monday – José Luis Padula, 1927)

Tango too had turned a corner – though it would encounter many more crossroads in its progress.

6 THE DYING OF THE LIGHT

Cuando la suerte qu' es grela,
fayando y fayando
te largue parao;
cuando estés bien en la vía,
sin rumbo, desesperao;
cuando no tengas ni fe,
ni yerba de ayer
secándose al sol;
cuando rajés los tamangos
buscando ese mango
que te haga morfar . . .
la indiferencia del mundo
– que es sordo y es mudo –
recién sentirás.

Verás que todo es mentira,
verás que nada es amor,
que al mundo nada le importa . . .
¡Yira!... ¡Yira! . . .
Aunque te quiebre la vida,
aunque te muerda un dolor,
no esperes nunca una ayuda,
ni una mano, ni un favor.

Cuando estén secas las pilas
de todos los timbres
que vos apretás,
buscando un pecho fraterno
para morir abrazao . . .
Cuando te dejen tirao
después de cinchar
lo mismo que a mí.
Cuando manyés que a tu lado
se prueban la ropa
que vas a dejar . . .
Te acordarás de este otario
que un día, cansado, ¡se puso a ladrar!

When fate, who is a woman / fails you time and again / and leaves you on your uppers / when you're set on your way / aimless and in despair / when you have nothing to believe in / nor even mate leaves / drying in the sun; / when you wear out your shoes / looking for cash / so that you can eat / you'll feel / the indifference of a world / that hears and says nothing.
Everything's a lie, you'll see / there's no love anywhere / the world doesn't give a damn / it just turns . . . and turns . . . / Your life can fall apart / the pain can eat into you / but don't expect anyone to help / to give you a hand, to do you a favour.
When there are only dead batteries / in every bell / you press / look-ing for a fraternal breast / to embrace before you die; / when they just leave you lying there / after all your efforts / like they did with me. / When you realize that they're standing next to you / trying on the clothes / you'll leave behind . . . You'll remember this fool / who, one day, exhausted / began to scream!
        ('Yira, yira', Turn, turn – Enrique Santos Discépolo, 1930)

Of all Santos Discépolo's lyrics, 'Yira, Yira' came to summarize what in *lunfardo* was called *la mishiadura*, loosely, 'the breadline'. For the people who gave birth to tango, the 1930s were hard times; unemployment rose dramatically and although Argentina did not suffer the world recession to the same depth as the United States, for example, there was hardship nevertheless, and '*la mishiadura*' was a reality for many. The bitterness of Discépolo's commentary strikes at the very heart of the notion of community on which the national imaginary was founded; a community based not so much on collective experience and solidarity as on a shared past. The implication was that the harsh life alluded to in every tango had not passed, but that its characteristic egoism and alienation had resurfaced in the face of the economic realities of the decade. That was why some called the Thirties in Argentina *la década infame*.

Gardel, of course, had sung all of Discépolo's lyrics. Yet his voice and the framing of the songs on screen in these early days of sound cinema attenuated the anger they contained. Gardel had come to occupy the pinnacle of the star system at this time of hardship and economic crisis and had offered a kind of consolation in the nostalgia that suffused his songs. The past recaptured provided perhaps an explanation of present difficulties. And at the same time, paradoxically, it offered a flawed utopia on which to look back with longing.

By mid-decade, a programme of public works launched the city into a second transformation as ambitious as the process that had taken the small town by the river and turned it into a second Paris on the River Plate forty or so years earlier. Like Brazil to the north, Argentina was announcing its emergence from the world recession and its aspirations for the future in an architectural vision. The future it envisaged would once again be based on its external trade and exports. It would remain, under the conservative governments of the time, as European in its culture and its horizons as those who launched Buenos Aires into the world. The new modernity was marked by the enormous breadth of the Avenida 9 de Julio (some fourteen lanes wide), which, like its counterparts at the turn of the century, swept away the narrow city centre streets of the past. The old church of St Nicholas fell to the bulldozers of a new age, to be replaced by Libertad Square and its emblematic central monument the needle of the Obelisk (both designed by Alberto Prebisch), which stretched its single arm into the sky and announced that Argentina was looking outside itself to a wider world. And most significantly, Corrientes Street, the main drag of the sexual city, was also widened as it had been during the city's first metamorphosis.

The project was imbued with a new moralism; the city's ambiguous attitude towards its own underworld was expressed in its repeated attempts to legislate its sex industry out of existence. In 1934, brothels were once again banned – a clear sign that the very similar law of 1919 had failed in its purposes. Now the cafés and cabarets became the meeting point for the women of the night and their clientele. And their trysts would be accompanied through the Thirties by the tango ensembles and singers displaced from the theatres by the advent of talking, or rather singing cinema. The bulk of Argentine cinema's production in its first decade were musicals,[1] building on Gardel's truncated singing career. The cast of the first national sound film, ¡Tango! (1933) would become the stars of the decade – Libertad Lamarque (until her very public falling out with Evita led her into exile and a highly successful singing career in Mexican cinema), Mercedes Simone, Tita Merello, as well as their male counterparts – Edgardo Donato, Osvaldo Fresedo and the dancer El Cachafaz, among others. Many of these early films reenacted tango stories, and their characters were certainly familiar from the lyrics of the Guardia Nueva.

This was the era of the women tango singers. Yet Rosita Quiroga, Ada Falcón, Azucena Maizani, or indeed Lamarque and Simone, did not change the grammar of tango. It was rare for them to sing from a woman's point of view; but there was an undoubted intended irony in their rendering of such intensely masculine feelings, feelings that Maizani ironized in her famous performance of 'Pero yo sé'.[2] But in their provocative and ironic use of words written for and by men, they offered some challenge, some instinct to transgress, some defiance against the fading of the light. Tita Merello's performance of 'Se dice de mí . . .' (People talk about me) is exemplary. On screen she sways and flirts, steering her course among the men laughing, slightly awkwardly, at the challenge she is offering. People say, she says, that 'my nose is too sharp and my figure wanting, that my mouth's too big and I'll always fight back'. So why is everyone so interested in this woman with nothing to offer? She might be ugly and everything that jealous women and spurned men might say about her, but they just keep coming back. 'Se dice de mi' (1943), though written by a man (Ivo Pelay), is a rare celebration of women's sexual power.

Proud and defiant, Merello's character remains the *milonguita* whose independence and scorn for the rules of bourgeois morality may well explain the enthusiasm of many Argentine women for her music, and for the tango in general. It was an answer to the moralism of the male view of the women they so easily condemned for their brief prosperity.

Gardel's reputation had largely been created outside the country. His early successes came in France and Spain, and later Hollywood relocated him in the artificial landscapes veiling the economic reality that it created so well. Once again, it seemed, tango returned to Buenos Aires flushed with success from Paris – and Hollywood.

But a new generation of singers and performers were emerging in the more restricted world of Buenos Aires and Montevideo. The reality is that there were fewer new lyricists emerging in this depression era;[3] Ignacio Corsini and Augustín Magaldi, and later Julio Sosa were taking to the stage, or more precisely to the corner daises of cafés and cabarets.

Musically, too, external realities pressed in on tango. Juan D'Arienzo, for example, expanded his ensemble to achieve the bigger sound to which cinema had accustomed audiences. Osvaldo Pugliese, a key figure from 1939 onwards, assembled his first orchestra in that year, and then created a sound that drew on influences beyond tango, particularly jazz. Carlos di Sarli, for his part, largely suppressed solos in his performances to give a lush and melodic collective sound – only the piano was given an individual voice. He was building on the work of Osvaldo Fresedo, one of tango's more adventurous musicians who experimented with new instruments, like the vibraphone. The decade ended, and the dancers were returning as the economy began to grow; Argentina's new industries were beginning to produce the goods that no longer reached her from the factories of Europe, now devoted to war production. And the expansion drew a new generation of immigrants, this time from the interior of the country and particularly the northwest. To a conservative ruling class in Buenos Aires, this new migration was deeply problematic. Once, many years before, their predecessors had welcomed the white-skinned populations who would both labour and Europeanize the emerging nation. But those who arrived seeking work in the new wartime industries were dark-skinned refugees from rural poverty – they called them, with deep racist contempt, the *cabecitas negras* ('black heads').

In the latter part of the 1930s, tango was stepping back into the limelight. As the decade ended, it was entering a new Golden Age. (Tango seems able to be endlessly reborn, rediscovered and reanimated by one generation after another. It is part of its magic).

The 1940s . . . witnessed the tango at the peak of its popularity. It was the centrepiece of the cabarets, the dance salons, the 'dancings', the cafes, the *confiterías* (pastry shops), the social and sports clubs and the soccer clubs. Newspapers now reserved several pages for advertisements for tango activities.[4]

Tango bands and orchestras multiplied, as did the venues where they played. Theatres were turned back into dance halls and concert stages; and many of the cafés on the iconic Corrientes Street divided their days into three or more sessions attended by different sections of the population to dance or to listen to the music.

Musically, the era was dominated by the extraordinary bandoneonista Aníbal Troilo, El Pichuco or El Gordo ('the Fat Man'). He led a large orchestra, a quartet, and accompanied some of the finest singers of the times – Francisco Fiorentino, Edmundo Rivero and others. His orchestra changed and matured, its instrumentation grew more complex, until it became 'a kind of colloquium of several voices, at times broken like a human voice, counterpoint and conflict . . . and later an ensemble chord'.[5]

Alfredo Gobbi, the son of a famous father who had been instrumental in taking tango to Paris at the turn of the century, developed a romantic style in his violin playing – and the rhythmic complexity of his arrangements moved him away from the dance-based bands like Juan D'Arienzo's, which, with Troilo, was the most popular and most dependable for the dance enthusiasts of the day.

This Golden Age also gave birth to a new kind of tango-song, more literary and metaphorical.

Just as the tango of the Twenties was linked to the imaginary of its time, the tango of the Forties turned its gaze back. It was untouched by the modifications in the city or it saw them with hostile eyes, full of suspicion and doubt.[6]

Anibal Troilo, 'El Pichuco'.

José María Contursi's immensely popular 'Sombras nada más' (1948) marks a transition – a passage in the tango drama from a luminous Golden Age to a more meditative evening in which shadows fall across the urban landscape of tango. The singer is an older man whose powers were inadequate to win the love of a woman obviously younger than himself. All that he can imagine now is cutting his wrists and watching the blood flow around her, and waiting until the shadows fall finally between them. Shadows 'between your love and mine', 'between your life and mine'. It is a familiar tango drama, but it may also be a metaphor for the distance that opened between tango and its origins.[7]

The 1940s, the decade in which this tango was completed, were the zenith of tango's popularity in Argentina and indeed across the world. The world it evoked and commemorated was fading from popular memory. Homero Manzi and Cátulo Castillo stand out as the poets of this era of regret for the passing of an age. Manzi's famous 'Malena', so often recorded by other artists since it was written in 1942, constructs a composite image of the ephemeral woman passing through the half dark to some transitory assignation, but now 'all the doors are closed to her'.

It is as if tango were fading into a mist, declining into nostalgia for a world that was full of disappointment, morally bereft and socially divided, yet which possessed a still living memory of a past beyond which lay a place of peace and harmonious relationships, where the natural order of things, overseen by a solicitous mother, was never truly disturbed. In this more recent, still-remembered past, sexuality dominated everything, yet as in the dance, it was an eroticism shot through with sadness, a sense of transience and disappointment. For some tango lyricists, this reflected a chaotic, dangerous and unstable modernity; for others, like Discépolo and Flores, that sense of loss was a feeling born of exploitation and powerlessness. 'Cambalache' was its most complete expression.

In either case, the gradual disappearance of *lunfardo* universalized that sense of loss.

PERÓN BRINGS BACK THE TANGO

In a small-town cabaret in the late Thirties, a young woman, the illegitimate daughter of a local politician, met with the famous singer Agustín Magaldi, then touring the provincial Argentina where he was enormously popular. Eva Duarte fascinated him, and he brought her back to Buenos Aires, where she sang with him and made minor inroads into film and radio soap opera. It was at the studios of Radio Belgrano in 1944, in fact, where she

Evita and Perón.

met Juan Domingo Perón, at that time Minister of Labour in the
government of General Pedro Ramírez. She was 25 years old. By
the time of her death, just eight years later, she would be a legend.[8]

It was to be expected that tango would be identified with the
period of change that ended so dramatically in 1930 with the coup
against Yrigoyen. The excluded new middle class and the emerging
working class had supported his Radical Party and undoubtedly
voted it into power. And however conflictive the relationship
between the immigrants and their children who were forging
the first trade unions in the country, the alternative was always
seen as a return to government by the fiercely anti-immigrant,
white landowning classes. It was these sections of the population
who were certainly behind the Uruburu coup of 1930, and who
re-entered power with him. Their hostility towards the immigrant
population, whom they relentlessly associated with moral decline
and criminality, was palpable. One result of their return to the pink
presidential palace in Buenos Aires was a new cultural campaign to
restore a European culture of the elite. They scorned tango, with
the result that the social dances which had flowered through the
1920s began to prove less popular, particularly with a middle class
anxious for respectability and furthermore suffering the reflected
impact of the Crash of 1929 and the worldwide recession that
followed. These were hard times for many, with unemployment
rising fast and the major social problems faced by the poorer
communities – housing above all – largely unresolved. The
reconstruction of the Buenos Aires city centre in mid-decade was
an echo of the strategy of restarting the economy through public
works. In fact, Argentina had suffered relatively less from the effects
of recession than other countries. Its industries had started to grow
in 1933, particularly in textiles and food.[9] The United Kingdom had
guaranteed the continuing import of Argentine beef in 1933,
although the agreement was less positive than it might have
appeared to be since the volume of imports was maintained at

1932 levels and the quid pro quo was to give privileged access to over 300 British imports into Argentina. But Argentina was nevertheless emerging from recession into an era of prosperity, with rising agricultural and industrial production. Even so, there as wide public resentment at what were seen to be excessive concessions to foreign companies, and the corruption that generally accompanied such deals.

The growth of Argentine industry brought 700,000 rural migrants, the *cabecitas negras* or *descamisados* (shirtless ones) to the cities and overwhelmingly to Buenos Aires. When the manufactured goods previously imported from Europe or the United States were no longer available, the industrial capacity to replace them with Argentine products already existed and expanded to fill the gap left.

At the same time, relations with the U.S. were deteriorating in an atmosphere of increasingly fervent nationalism. This did not necessarily find favour among the first or second generation immigrant communities whose cultural and ideological links with the old countries remained very strong and were sustained through community and trade union organizations. Anarchism retained its influence among them with its resolutely internationalist perspective and its deep distrust of governments. As the Second World War began, Argentine nationalism was largely a conservative force in the country. And when, in the aftermath of Pearl Harbor and the USA's entry into the war, Argentina refused to enter into its Pan-American alliances, the U.S.government responded by withholding arms sales and increasing weapons exports to Brazil, which the Argentines interpreted as a direct threat. An agreement between Argentina and the U.S. in October 1941 offered little more than token changes, fanning anti-U.S. feelings. The German government was watching these events closely and intensifying its propaganda activities in Argentina, where it found a resonance in government circles dominated by anti-semitism, anti-communism and a deeply conservative religiosity. Washington was quick to denounce the government in Buenos Aires as pro-Nazi. This only served to provoke and intensify local nationalism. The 1943 film *El fin de la noche* included a performance of Discépolo's 'Uno' ('One' or 'You') by Libertad Lamarque; it was banned by the military government of Ramon S. Castillo. The tango itself, with music by Mariano Mores, was also suppressed and denied access to radio. At first sight this may seem to be one more ballad of disappointed love; but it is more profound than that, as an expression of the desolation that real poverty brings. More than that, it speaks of *desarraigo*, the sense of not belonging that informed tango from its beginnings and that now returns against the background of a repressive and hostile government – 'dragging yourself over thorns', echoing the promise of utopia in the life beyond that religion offers. But the price is very high – 'you give your life for a kiss that never comes', a kiss that is the end of hunger, the hope of a decent life. The theme here is not just the search for one passionate encounter but for a warmth that ends 'this cruel cold that is worse than hate' and leads only to 'the awful tomb where love lies'. This is more than disappointment in love – it is the betrayal of the promise that decades earlier had brought hopeful immigrants to the port of Buenos Aires.

In June 1943 a military coup again ousted the government, though the army command was politically divided over what should follow. One faction advocated a more liberal and conciliatory approach to trade with the north. Another, gathered in the United Officers Group or 'GOU', advocated economic nationalism and anti-communism. The attempt by the moderates to reach an agreement with the U.S. to lift the arms embargo in exchange for a break with the Axis Powers met an obdurate refusal in Washington.

Colonel Juan Domingo Perón,[10] a military officer with close ties to Mussolini's Italy, rose rapidly in the new government, first as War Minister and then in the enormously powerful Ministry of Labour. In the course of his road to power, he changed political direction and began to identify himself with the new immigrants from the countryside, the *descamisados*. His wife, Evita, was an enormous help in his campaign for the presidency. She was a singer of tangos and ballads, the protégée of the much-loved performer Magaldi, and a woman from a poor provincial family, not to mention an actress in the highly popular *radionovelas*, the radio soap operas – she was, in a word, like them. And Perón, in building his devoted base of support among the new workers, exploited her ability to appeal to them. They were not welcomed into the existing trade unions, and they were socially marginalized as recent rural migrants to the big city which earlier generations of immigrants had appropriated for themselves. Arrested by the military government in 1945, Perón was released into the arms of tumultuous waiting crowds. He and Evita addressed them from the presidential balcony in the language of the street, and to the delight of some of tango's most prominent musicians – Discépolo and Homero Manzi among them. Indeed, Manzi wrote two songs for Perón and Evita.

Tango and its musicians, like Argentine society itself, was deeply divided by their attitude to Perón. And this was further complicated by the hostility of the Argentine Communist Party towards him. The reasons were complex: the party was conservative and cautious and deeply suspicious of Perón's mix of populism and anti-communism. And the hostility was echoed by Perón himself. One of tango's outstanding exponents, the pianist Osvaldo Pugliese, was a communist who was jailed under both Perón and the right-wing government that overthrew and succeeded him. Yet Pugliese was one of tango's great survivors and re-emerged with it when it had its second renaissance at the hands of Astor Piazzola.

In 1943, Hugo Wast (nom de plume of Gustavo Martínez Zuviria), Minister of Education of the military regime, had set up a 'purification commission' with the enthusiastic support of the Archbishop of Buenos Aires. Its aim was to 'purify' the language of its '*lunfardo* elements' and some of the linguistic echoes that linked it to the immigrant past, in particular the use of the anachronistic 'vos' pronoun instead of the intimate and polite forms approved by the Spanish Royal Academy, 'tú' and 'usted'. It was a direct assault on the tango and, more indirectly, a challenge to the cosmopolitan and *mestizo* version of Argentine nationalism. Not for the first time, or the last, tango's references and collective memory would present an image of the nation that conservatives found unacceptable. Just as the original leaders of a unified Argentina had worked to purge it of Indian resonances and black cultural residues in the mid-nineteenth century, each conservative regime thereafter fought to restore a vision of Argentine nationhood that was white, Catholic, and resolutely Hispanic in the mould of the grand families whose defiantly Mediterranean mansions can still be found in the Florida district of the city. The same battle had recommenced in the post-radical governments after 1930, from Uruburu onwards. And the confrontation would be deliberately renewed in the most murderous terms by the military government of the 1960s and 1970s, insistent as always on a Christian heritage that was racist, anti-semitic and unashamedly elitist.

Through the 1930s, tango had reflected and voiced the frustration and anger of ordinary people faced with a regime at once corrupt and brutal. At the same time, it provided a momentary refuge. The lyrics of Enrique Santos Discépolo and Celedonio Flores were its expression. The gains made for working people – especially in terms of political representation – were embodied in the Yrigoyen regime, at least in its early phases. And in some sense, it was the memory of that time – idealized perhaps – that Perón evoked, for an expanded urban population of new immigrants and old. If the *década infame* inaugurated by the military regime of Uruburu, which began in 1930, had been 'a time of profound collective and individual frustration and humiliation' for working-class people,[11] Perón not only addressed directly the economic needs of the new rural immigrants, his beloved *descamisados* – he also promised a concept of nationhood and citizenship which specifically embraced all the working people of Argentina, *el pueblo trabajador* who occupied such a central place in his discourse.

As some commentators were quick to underline, there could be no Peronist tango as such. Though their arguments often derived from a bitter hostility to Perón from the conservative right or from the communists, who were as ferociously opposed to him as those on the opposite side of the spectrum, there was a point of substance in what they were saying. Tango's origins, its history and its narrative were rooted in a community that was marginalized and excluded. In that sense, Gardel's recreation of the tango hero, while it placed tango at the very heart of popular culture, also romanticized it and sweetened its bitter edge. It was the words and music of Celedonio Flores and Discépolo which provided the soundtrack of the era from the perspective of those who had given the tango birth. The infinite geography of the body, its movements and its hidden depths and possibilities, stood for the geography of the wider world in which the characters of this urban drama still had no place.

If, as Perón increasingly claimed when he was in power, he had invited the working class in from the cold, and if the depression era was now to give way to prosperity and full employment, how could tango – as the poetry of urban alienation – survive the transition? For some of the key figures of tango, like Discépolo himself and Homero Manzi, Perón was the salvation of Argentina and Evita the iconic symbol of the tango generations that had gone before. Indeed, Evita was the link between past and future. Her story, at least as it was retold, was an archetypal tango story, beginning with her background in poverty (albeit in the provinces), then her affair with the tango singer Magaldi, and then her rapid ascent to the world of diamonds and furs which she so elegantly carried (much to the disgust not only of Argentina's traditional oligarchic families but also of the royal families of Spain and Britain whose noses were permanently put out of joint by her vulgar insistence on being treated like one of them). This was a story endlessly retold in the idiom of tango. Yet Hugo del Carril's eulogies to both Perón and Evita (with music by Homero Manzi) did little justice to the poetry of tango. In form he returned to the tradition of the *payador*, whose improvised verses had always marked civic occasions, public scandals, or retold the endless fables of rural life. Carril's fervid praise of the new golden couple, Juan Perón and Evita, were public anthems which won him what proved to be only temporary access to the higher echelons and threw a veil across his musical career. And Enrique Maroni's *La descamisada*, famously sung by Nelly Omar, was one of a number of enthusiastic oaths of loyalty to Evita – in effect a campaign song for the 'mother of the nation'.

In fact, the period of Perón divided the tango community. His most fervent adherents, like Manzi and particularly Hugo del Carril, were mistreated and rejected. The comments on Hugo del Carril's 'Los muchachos peronistas' were at best scathing, so it is particularly poignant that del Carril so offended Evita, in ways still unspecified, that it would be many years before the official composer of *Peronismo* would receive the plaudits of his home city. While at the time, some musicians baulked at the limitations imposed by Perón's labour laws, and generally stood aside from politics, they participated cheerfully in the tango boom that Perón oversaw. Perón himself was happy to be seen with the tango greats, and in March 1949, finally lifted the ban on *lunfardo* and the censorship of tango lyrics imposed by the military government some six years before. And tango basked in what remained of its second Golden Age.

7 ASTOR PIAZZOLA AND TANGO NUEVO

THE DANCING COMES TO AN END

Peronism led the working class of Argentina half way to the top of a hill between 1946 and 1951. Evita's promise of a radical new vision seemed briefly on the horizon. There was full employment, wages rose, the trade unions came to occupy a central place in Argentine society under Peronist tutelage. And the frustration and discontent of Argentine's wealthy classes confirmed in a negative way that real change was under way.[1] In 1947 and 1948 several major industries and companies were brought under public control; the railways were nationalized, so too were the national oil company and the utility and telephone companies. Perón's rise to power derived from the alliances he forged from the Ministry of Labour with the trade union leaders; it was they who mobilized the massive demonstration of 17 October 1945 which brought Perón and Evita back to centre stage and prepared the way for his presidential victory the following year in 1946.[2]

Given the position Argentina had taken during the war period, and Perón's openly nationalistic stance together with his earlier sympathy for Mussolini, it is perhaps not surprising that the United States should take the openly hostile attitude towards him that they did. The famous Blue Book, prepared by u.s. ambassador Braden, ostensibly demonstrated Perón's contacts with European fascism and underpinned Washington's continuing attacks on him. Surprisingly, perhaps, the Argentine Communist Party supported that position and also denounced Perón as a fascist. Yet from the point of view of the workers, Perón was championing their cause, and as president was pushing through legislation in favour of the masses. And his political language, his discourse, returned endlessly to his sympathy with the workers and his desire to speak for and represent 'the people', which Evita articulated and reinforced.

There are many ways to describe Perón's political position[3] – but what is clear is that he succeeded in forging a kind of consensus around the symbolism of nationhood and the improvement of the living standards of the majority. During his first presidency, wages rose for both skilled and unskilled workers. The *aguinaldo* or 'thirteenth month' (an extra month's payment at the end of the year) was introduced, together with pensions, sick and holiday pay, and new rules over health and safety at work. The trade unions opened holiday camps, sports centres and built houses for workers. It was these years that created the myth of Peronism that has sustained the Peronist tradition ever since. All this was financed by new industrialization measures and a public sector whose coffers were swollen by rising agricultural production.

And tango too was a beneficiary. In part, the tango musicians were aided by Perón's commitment to national culture – but it was not the only one. The *cabecitas negras* brought their own music, the 'folklore' or folk music represented by Atahualpa Yupanqui and Jorge Cafrune, for example, which was still extremely popular in the interior of the country. Yet there was no clear division between the two audiences; both the new immigrants and the children of earlier generations crowded into the sports clubs and dance halls to hear tango and dance. And even as they were doing so, in the prosperous and optimistic times of the late Forties, tango itself was dividing between the musicians who played for dancing and those who saw tango as a broader musical genre evolving and merging with other forms (they called themselves the 'evolutionists').

In 1951 Perón was re-elected; in February 1952 Evita died of leukaemia. All cinema showings were stopped and the announcement made: 'at 8.25 this evening the lady passed into eternal life'. By now, an economic crisis loomed, and Perón turned against his allies in the working-class movement. Strikes were broken and demonstrations attacked. Living standards and wage levels began to decline. And conservative Argentina – the Church, the upper echelons of the military and the business organizations which had benefited considerably during the early part of Perón's regime now turned against him – together with the Communist Party.

Perón had his allies among the tango community, above all Discépolo and Homero Manzi and, until he was disgraced, Hugo del Carril. Only Osvaldo Pugliese was an active opponent, as a communist, and he was to suffer for it. As the atmosphere changed in the latter years of Perón's regime, the memory of Evita came to stand for a collective nostalgia for a Peronism remembered and idealized. The reality, however, was a reversal of what had gone before – major companies were sold back to their original owners, trade unions now actively controlled and repressed their own more militant members, while rising inflation generated an increasing dissatisfaction.

The great orchestras were beginning to disband as the venues of tango's second Golden Age began to close. And, in 1955, Perón was overthrown in a military coup that began in the city of Córdoba and spread rapidly through the country. It was the second attempt to bring him down; the first, in August, had left hundreds dead in the Plaza de Mayo of Buenos Aires. Despite rumours to the contrary, there was only minimal mass resistance to the September coup at the time, and Perón himself basically walked away. The leader of what was called the 'Liberating Revolution', *la Revolución Libertadora*, was General Lonardi, a nationalist who was willing to leave in place some of the advances made under Perón, under the slogan 'Neither victor nor defeated'. It may be that this is what persuaded the Peronist organizations that they were safe.[4] Nonetheless, within weeks there were strikes and demonstrations and armed resistance from the more militant sections, as the nature of the new regime rapidly became clear. The response was repressive and brutal, as Lonardi was replaced by the hardline Aramburu.

The immigrants of 60 and 70 years earlier were part of the 'Peronist Resistance' (as these years of social conflict and struggle came to be called). The vision they were fighting to defend, of a cosmopolitan nation enshrined in the tango, now faced more than a decade of political instability, state violence and repression by a succession of military governments interspersed with civilian regimes all heavily dependent on the armed forces.[5]

In the era that followed tango's Golden Age of dance and the Perón period, Argentina sank into over two decades of repression and fear. The latter part of the Fifties was shaped by the long resistance against the military and civilian coalitions that ruled implacably after the departure of Lonardi in 1956. The country prospered, its industries expanded; but the political conditions of existence were forged by the ceaseless struggle between government and a trade union movement largely operating underground and dominated, at least initially, by the Peronist leaders who had come to control them during the 1945–55 decade.

The underground resistance surfaced time and again, and always with a political demand for the return of Perón, who was living in Spain. In a sense, the Peronism that prevailed in Argentina among those who opposed the governments that succeeded him was not one idea but many – though each claimed legitimacy by reference to the symbolism of Evita. The battle for possession of her body was a political argument conducted as ritual. At one level, Peronism was defined in practice as an ideology of militant trade unionism which was itself divided between the old trade union bureaucracy using their influence to win political recognition for

Peronism, and a new emerging militant trade unionism rooted
in factory-based rank and file movements which was readier to
confront repressive government through street struggles and
factory occupations. In 1962, the government of Arturo Illía moved
towards recognition of Peronism and the possibility that the
movement could participate in official political life. But Perón
himself was still not allowed to return. A general strike called by
the leaders of the official trade union majority in December 1965
demanding the right of return for Perón had only a patchy response,
and accelerated the internal divisions within the movement. But it
seemed increasingly likely that the presidential elections of 1967
would produce a Peronist majority. The army moved to overthrow
the government in a pre-emptive strike. The new president, General
Onganía, belonged to a group implacably opposed to Peronism and
committed to long-term government by the military.

The extraordinary thing is that the new government was
supported by the Peronists and enjoined by their exiled leader to
sit back and wait.[6] Yet Onganía's regime proved very quickly to be
bitterly hostile to working-class interests. Its early economic policies
clearly favoured foreign capital and the export industries and included cutbacks and a wage freeze. The years 1967–72 involved increasing
confrontation, militant working-class activities culminating in the
two *Cordobazos*, and the city-wide strikes in Cordoba in 1969 and
1971, during which its working class seized control of the city. As
Onganía gave way to generals Levingston and Lanusse, the social
conflict – and the repression – deepened dramatically. The Peronist
movement was divided and many sections of the movement were
now looking to a more far-reaching transformation, and adding
methods of armed struggle to working-class militancy.

By 1972, it was clear to General Lanusse that it would be
impossible to restore social order without the influence of Perón.
He returned, with his new wife María Isabel ('Isabelita'), late in
1972. But if the military hoped that a new consensus would

emerge, they were mistaken. The firefight that broke out as Perón left Ezeiza Airport resulted in over a hundred dead, signalling the times to come. And Isabelita was not Evita. Her relationship with Perón's secretary, López Rega, was intimate and corrupt, as would soon emerge. The years of military government had also been a period of deepening social conflict during which new forms of popular organization had emerged in Córdoba, Mendoza and elsewhere – and when the language of politics now included the possibility of a revolutionary change. Sections of Peronism were now committed to the overthrow of the regime and in this they joined with other Left organizations for whom the moment also represented a revolutionary crisis.

Under Perón, the traditional tango had reached a kind of stasis. Leading lyricists and musicians, like Discépolo and Manzi, gave much of their time to politics. And there was, of course, a deeper contradiction. The tango of the 1930s was a bitter commentary on a society in an economic crisis in which most people were experiencing severe difficulties and many had lost their jobs, their hope and their optimistic vision of the national future. The tango of the 1920s had created a kind of national myth, a shared past out of which emerged the cosmopolitan image of the capital city. The 1930s were best summarized by Discépolo's 'Qué Vachaché', which had proved so unpopular on its first performance in 1926, yet was taken up enthusiastically by the tango audience ten years later, when it reflected more precisely its discontents. Celedonio Flores's. 'Pan' (Bread) described the actions of some of the city's poor in attacking a bakery:

> ¿Adónde? ¿Trabajar? ¿Extender la mano
> pidiendo, al que pasa, limosna? ¿Por qué?
> ¿Recibir la afrenta de un perdón hermano; . . .
> . . . Se durmieron todos, cachó la barreta
> ¡Si Jesús no ayuda, que ayude Satán!

Un vidrio, unos gritos, auxilio, carreras . . .
¡un hombre que llora y un cacho de pan!

Work? Where? Holding out your hand / Asking passing strangers for
a coin? Why? / Facing the offence of a 'sorry pal'? . . . / Everyone's
asleep now, he grabs the iron bar / If Jesus won't help then the Devil
will / A pane of glass, shouting, help, running feet . . . / A weeping
man and a crust of bread.

('Pan', Bread – Celedonio Flores, 1933)

Tango in the early Thirties had embraced protest, speaking
on behalf of the very same diverse public who for a while had felt
fully integrated into the national community and reflected in the
collective psyche. A decade later those sections of society again
found themselves excluded by a renewed appeal to the most
conservative of Hispanic Christian values.

Perón restored their faith, perhaps. But the new immigrants
from the rural interior were problematic, and the older urban
community was divided in its reaction. The new arrivals from the
country came with their own musical identity, their own dances,
their own shared memory. Born in the province of Mendoza in
1913, Antonio Tormo was a well-known and popular radio artist
in provincial Argentina before arriving in the capital in 1947 – a
significant moment. His songs, like the huge bestseller 'El rancho
e la cambiche', spoke of rural life and the favourite dance of the
Argentine northwest, the *chamame*, a traditional couple dance
accompanied by guitars played in the style of the ancient *vihuela*.
The scattered words in the Guarani language of the Paraguayan
frontier functioned just as *lunfardo* had done in the tango – to
symbolize a different life and a different history.[7] Yet Tormo had
to acknowledge tango in the lyrics of the song.

Perón's conscious and sophisticated deployment of that shared
past resonated with his supporters among the recent working-class

arrivals from the north. And his support for 'national' music embraced both the rural and the urban traditions. Tango now had to share the public musical space. And, in fact, many tango musicians chose not to give their support to Perón but instead to play for the still enthusiastic dancing public. The number of lyricists declined.

> Tango was facing its sunset, reiterating old issues, interpellating people who did not exist any more, making remembrance of the past its major theme. It was so fixed in its old structures that the most important tango poets of the period, who were also supporters of Perón, were unable to link their lyrics with the new social process that was occurring.[8]

Homero Manzi's 'Sur', written in 1947, might serve as an epitaph, just as it did for the great musician himself, who died shortly after its composition. The music was by the other great survivor of the Golden Age, Aníbal Troilo. It is a string of memories – the shop on the corner, the muddy streets, the smell of alfalfa, the barrios, like Pompeya, where tango was born: 'Nostalgia for the things that have passed on / grains of sand that life blew away'. And sadness that it should all have disappeared, except in memory.

As we have seen, it was the old tango that died; the new was just emerging in new ways and new places.

In many ways, the regimes that followed Perón were united by the deeply conservative vision that time and again had confronted and challenged the concept of the nation as a melting pot of cultures, traditions and histories – a concept embedded deeply in the tango.

Cátulo Castillo s 'La última curda' feels like an elegy, or perhaps an epitaph, for the *compadrito*. His woman companion is tango itself. And it serves, by date and register, to mark the beginning of an end. This final 'binge' (*curda*) unfolds against a grey background and a fading past. The 'dancings' had mostly closed, few of the *confiterías* and cafés were left, the sports clubs could no longer afford the spectacular Saturday gatherings they had organized through the late Forties. In the venues that remained a different music was heard and it was listened to in a different way. Small ensembles replaced the ambitiously large orchestras of the previous time; they played what was now called *tango de cámara*, or 'chamber tango'. They were musically adventurous and engaged with other musics and traditions in enormously creative ways. The artists from previous generations that continued playing, chief among them the great Aníbal Troilo, were largely disapproving of this *tango nuevo* (new tango). It was not danceable, it was avant-garde, it was fluid and open. It broke with the tango tradition. It welcomed the influence of jazz, of black music, of elements of the classical repertoire. Yet this was tango still, and the era of chamber tango produced some of the greatest individual virtuosi in the tradition, most of whom had learned their craft with Manzi, Troilo, Pugliese and Caló – the outstanding figures of the *Guardia Nueva* and the Golden Age. They included Roberto Grela on guitar, Horacio Salgán and Juan José Paz on piano, Enrique Mario Francini on violin, Pedro Laurenz and Pedro Maffia on bandoneon. There were others, of course; but for all of them the small ensembles playing in the cafés were an opportunity to play for a public growing accustomed to listening rather than dancing.

ASTOR PIAZZOLLA

One of the finest musicians of them all was Astor Piazzolla, bandoneon player, composer and arranger. When he went to Paris to work with the world famous piano teacher Nadia Boulanger, with the aim of becoming a classical musician, Boulanger commented that his classical playing lacked 'feeling' and asked him to play his own music. When he played tango on his bandoneon, she was emphatic: 'That's Piazzolla; never leave it'.

He would go on to revolutionize the music he loved, in his own compositions and arrangements and later in his remarkable collaborations with the Uruguayan poet and lyricist Horacio Ferrer.

Born in 1921, Piazzolla spent his childhood with his family in New York.[9] At the age of twelve he met Carlos Gardel and even played for him; indeed he appears as a newspaper boy in Gardel's film *El día que me quieras*. The family returned to Argentina, to Mar del Plata, in 1937, much against Astor's wishes – Spanish was still his second language. Buenos Aires was where the music was, of course; it was where he could listen to the newly formed orchestra of Aníbal Troilo and hear the bandoneon masters Pedro Maffia and Pedro Laurenz, the extraordinary but ill-starred pianist Orland Goñi, as well as the inimitable Fat Man. But a major influence on him seems to have been an ensemble which has left no recordings – Elvino Vardaro's Sextet. Astor would move restlessly from café to café, listening to the enormous variety of interpretations that were available in what was probably the richest musical period in tango's history. It was also, of course, a time of division between the traditionalists whose orchestras played for dancing and the experimental and avant-garde musicians, like Vardaro and Goñi, who were developing a music to be heard. Troilo, with whom Astor began his playing career, was a great admirer of the young man's talents, but he also warned him not to go beyond 'playing the music'. The difference between the two men was not simply about music. Troilo was not only the outstanding musician of 'traditional' tango, he was also the embodiment of the tango life. His girth testified to his love of good food and drink, and he spent a good part of his life in the clubs and cafés of the tango world. He tried hard to encourage Astor to follow him around the nightclubs of Corrientes Street but Astor was resistant. He was not much of a sybarite and no great lover of the smoky bars where the musicians went after their gigs. He would

Astor Piazzolla.

detach himself from Troilo and go home, getting up early to go to his classes with the great Argentine composer Alberto Ginestera, who taught him harmony and composition.

All these different influences could not but impel Astor towards experimentation and the fusion of styles and traditions. And he was surrounded by innovative musicians who encouraged him in this, albeit with the disapproval of his bandoneon master Aníbal Troilo, though Troilo continued to work with and support him.

In 1946, Piazzolla formed his first band and recorded its first album. But in 1949 it was dissolved when a phone call from the presidential palace instructed him to attend to play for Perón and his entourage. Rather than be compromised, Piazzolla informed the presidential palace that his band no longer existed.

The experience appears to have caused a degree of depression in him, and for the next few years he played less and devoted himself to composition; he was composing in a classical mould, and it was in that frame of mind that in 1954 he took up the opportunity of a scholarship to study in Paris with Nadia Boulanger. It was the great veteran teacher, whose list of pupils read like a catalogue of modernist music, who encouraged him to go back to tango.

Returning from Paris, Piazzolla launched the 'tango revolution' with a manifesto, his *Decálogo*.[10] The ensemble would 'be *listened* to by the public, it will not play at dances'. It would use a range of new instruments, and would work from scores; there would be no improvisation. The overall purpose was:

> to raise the quality of tango, to convince those who have moved away from the tango, and its detractors, of the unquestionable value of our music . . . to conquer the mass public . . . and to take tango abroad, as a musical ambassador . . . .

The rather dry and earnest tone of the *Decálogo* belies the daring and excitement of the music itself.

There is a case for viewing the Octet as the most audacious of Piazzolla's various ensembles. For the first time, Piazzolla treated all his musicians as solo instrumentalists. He allowed the electric guitar a high degree of improvisation, something totally unknown in previous tango music. The piano's free-flowing role, the counterpoint achieved with the strings, the percussive effects created by the strings and electric guitar, and the neatly calculated dissonances, gave the ensemble a revolutionary sound.[11]

The group played mainly for radio and in concert venues; it was emphatically not going to play to accompany singers. But in the context of Perón's recent overthrow and the shrinking space for tango music, this controversial music attracted limited interest, and few of the musicians could make a living playing it. By the end of 1957, Astor had decided to return to New York.

There was a logic in the trip beyond simply returning to his childhood home. Piazzolla's music was profoundly Argentine, but it had absorbed key elements from jazz. During the Octet's brief life, Piazzolla, its leader, acknowledged a special debt to Osvaldo Pugliese, who had drawn into his playing elements of black culture, the rhythms of African dance and the improvised shapes of jazz. Pugliese's 'La Yumba' and his key composition 'Malandraca' anticipated and informed the new tango, introducing jazz rhythms and syncopations which were in their turn a homage to the hidden origins of tango in black music. It seemed appropriate that the Octet should go to Pugliese to ask whether what they were doing was tango. Pugliese answered with an emphatic 'yes'.

Things did not go well for Astor in New York; he became a working musician playing more conventional tango and his own work went into a kind of hiatus. Then, in October 1959, his beloved father, his *nonino*, died. From his pain and sadness emerged what he himself, as well as many others regard as his finest piece – 'Adiós

Nonino'. Its core, and its opening, is a cheerful tango he had written in 1954, called simply 'Nonino'. Then in an abrupt change of tone, the original tune is taken up by an elegiac violin and continued in piano passages in dialogue with Piazzolla's bandoneon. It is a conversation around shared memories evoked in the music. And to watch Piazzolla playing the piece, is to see how his relationship with the bandoneon adds to the music a kind of choreographed embrace, as if bandoneon and player were sharing the pain of loss.[12] Carefully constructed like all his pieces, it nevertheless allows space for interpretation and self-expression for the extraordinary musicians with whom he worked. It also offers a narrative that has the insolent swing of the original tango interwoven with a lament and contemplative, and sometimes angry, interventions from the bandoneon. 'Adios Nonino' is a piece that has been recorded by an infinity of ensembles – though his own favourite was the version played by the Quintet which he formed on his return to Buenos Aires in 1960. He was resolved, as he expressed it at the time, to 'win the battle of tango nuevo', to establish its incontestable musical credentials. He composed relentlessly – some 1,000 pieces in all before his death in 1992. And he introduced into his new tango elements of every musical tradition: the harmonic progressions of jazz, the rhythmic phrasing of black music, the ground bass of Bach, the dissonances of Bartók, the impressionism of Debussy. Tango could absorb them all, just as it had integrated so many earlier traditions into its original sound.

An encounter with the Uruguayan poet Horacio Ferrer[13] opened new horizons for Piazzolla. Their collaboration over twenty years enjoyed huge early success with the 'Balada de un loco' (The Ballad of a Crazy Man). It was written for the Buenos Aires Festival of Song and Dance in November 1969, and won second prize and a very cool reception. Yet within a week the recording had sold 200,000 copies. Some said that it had not won first prize because of the resistance of a tango establishment that

was and remained bitterly hostile to Piazzolla's revolution
in tango.

Ya sé que estoy piantao, piantao, piantao . . .
No ves que va la luna rodando por Callao;
que un corso de astronautas y niños, con un vals,
me baila alrededor . . . ¡Bailá! ¡Vení! ¡Volá!

Ya sé que estoy piantao, piantao, piantao . . .
Yo miro a Buenos Aires del nido de un gorrión;
y a vos te vi tan triste . . . ¡Vení! ¡Volá! ¡Sentí! . . .
el loco berretín que tengo para vos:

¡Loco! ¡Loco! ¡Loco!
Cuando anochezca en tu porteña soledad,
por la ribera de tu sábana vendré
con un poema y un trombón
a desvelarte el corazón.

¡Loco! ¡Loco! ¡Loco!
Como un acróbata demente saltaré,
sobre el abismo de tu escote hasta sentir
que enloquecí tu corazón de libertad . . .
¡Ya vas a ver!

Quereme así, piantao, piantao, piantao . . .
Trepate a esta ternura de locos que hay en mí,
ponete esta peluca de alondras, ¡y volá!
¡Volá conmigo ya! ¡Vení, volá, vení!
Quereme así, piantao, piantao, piantao . . .
Abrite los amores que vamos a intentar
la mágica locura total de revivir . . .
¡Vení, volá, vení!

*I know I'm crazy, crazy, crazy / Can't you see the moon moving
along Callao Street / And a cortege of astronauts and children,
waltzing / Around me . . . Dance! Come! Fly!*

*I know I'm crazy . . . / I look down on Buenos Aires from a sparrow's
nest / and I saw you looking sad . . . Come! Fly! Feel! / this crazy gift
I have for you.*

*Mad! mad! mad! / When night falls on your Buenos Aires solitude /
I'll skirt the banks of your sheet / with a poem and a trombone /
and unveil your heart.*

*Mad! mad! mad! / I'll jump like a demented acrobat / over the
canyon of your decolleté until I feel / that I've driven you mad with
freedom in your heart / You'll see! . . .*

*Love me like this, crazy, crazy, crazy . . . / climb into this tenderness
of madmen there are in me / put on this wig of swallows and fly /
Fly with me, come, fly, come / Love me this way, crazy, crazy / Open
yourself to the love we'll soon attempt / the magical madness of
being born again. / Come! Fly! Come!*

('Balada de un loco', Ballad of a Crazy Man
– Piazzolla / Ferrer, 1969)

Ferrer had been true to the spirit of tango and revived its
language – *lunfardo*. But his lyrics were poetry in their own right,
a succession of surreal images and flights of fancy matched by the
soaring accompaniments that pressed both words and music into
new and unexpected combinations. Two years earlier, what they
called their 'little opera', *María de Buenos Aires*, had failed to make
a mark. But the 'Balada' , still a favourite across the world, struck
a chord with an audience that was reported to have received the
music in stunned (but, as it turned out, appreciative) silence. Many
of their joint compositions are futuristic, some apocalyptic, but
most revisited the cityscape of early tango with an ironic eye.
Ferrer saw Poe, Baudelaire and the Nicaraguan founder of Latin
American Modernism, Rubén Darío, as his influences: 'they travel

the deep, nocturnal, lower depths of the city'.[14] Clearly, Ferrer saw himself like Baudelaire's 'flaneur'; embedded in the city crowds, aimless and adrift in the streets of the modern metropolis, just as his predecessors watched from the shadows behind the streetlamps as the prostitutes and their clients passed by on their ephemeral journeys.

In 1970, Piazzolla returned to Paris; two years later he played in Buenos Aires's iconic Teatro Colón with a number of other tango orchestras. It was highly significant that tango itself, and even more so this brash and adventurous new variant, should find its way into Argentina's premier concert hall; it was a massive step towards recognition. But a heart attack in 1973 was taken as a warning that he should reduce the intensity of his working life. He found stability in Italy, where he lived for five years (1974–9), composing film music and recording several albums including the highly successful *Libertango*.[15] In those years he was drawn to electronic instrumentation and the possibilities of rock, forming his '*Conjunto Electrónico*'. The next ten years would be his most successful. His score for the film *El Exilio de Gardel (Tangos)* won him a César, and his ever widening corps of collaborators now included the jazz musician Gary Burton and the pianist and orchestra director Lalo Schifrin. In 1987, he returned to New York to record the album *Tango: Zero Hour* and to play a concert in Central Park in front of 4,000 people. New York had finally taken him to its heart. He went on to tour Europe before a heart attack in 1990 curtailed his extraordinary career.

It was fitting that Piazzolla's final years should have been attended with the success and acknowledgment in his own country which had been denied him for so long. His music for Fernando Solanas's iconic film *Sur* came to express the pain of exile and exclusion that the Argentine dancers living in Paris in *El Exilio de Gardel (Tangos)* set out to express in dance. It may be, paradoxically, that the impact of the stage show *Tango Argentino* across the world,[16] beginning in 1984, which featured so much of his work, propelled him into this new realm of global fame. By the late 1980s, it was impossible to sit in a modern café anywhere without hearing his music around you.

Throughout his life, Piazzolla sought and created a fusion, or perhaps a better term would be a creative 'encounter' between classical music, jazz, electronic music and tango. What he achieved was innovative, entirely original, moving and inspiring music. While his detractors denounced him for departing from tango or diluting it, in fact, the driving force within his work was always tango that was strengthened rather than denied by its meetings with other traditions. That is why the innumerable artists who have reinter-preted Piazzolla have never suppressed, even had they wanted to, the towering presence of tango at its heart.

A stroke in 1990 left those nimble, restless hands immobile and Piazzolla never returned to the bandoneon.

The last work he was to hear, 'Le grand tango', was written for and performed by the cello virtuoso Mstislav Rostropovich. Piazzolla's work had by then moved into a realm that embraced classical forms among its many references. Whether it was *tango nuevo* or a new music rooted in tango continues be a question for heated debate. What is certain is that he transformed the musical landscape of his country for ever, taking tango into new terrains and new encounters that angered purists but also freed tango from a dependence on its past and carried it triumphantly into new fusions and new arenas.

8 THE LONG ROAD HOME

EXILE AND RETURN

The second presidency of Juan Domingo Perón lasted less than a year before his death in July 1974. The shootout at the airport when he arrived a year earlier proved to be a sign of things to come. The interpretations of Perón's first regime produced very different and conflicting conclusions about what his return would mean. The rank and file of the working-class movement took it as a signal to radicalize their activities in a battle to restore the living standards and working conditions that had deteriorated so dramatically under the previous military regime.

In the elections of February 1973, Héctor Cámpora, a loyal supporter of the old man, was elected to the presidency. But he was always going to a be simple caretaker until Perón himself was allowed to return as a candidate for the presidency. When he did return, in September 1973, Perón was elected with 62 per cent of the popular vote. However, his movement was deeply divided politically and at war with itself. While Perón himself favoured a kind of social contract between trade unions and employers, the radical Left Peronists – led by the movement called the 'Montoneros' – spoke openly of a revolution. And the Perón of 1974 was not the man who had come to power thirty years earlier. There was no Evita at his side, and the new wife, Isabelita, who aspired to take over her role, had neither a mass base nor the charisma of her predecessor. In fact, she was under the sway of a small, corrupt and extremely right-wing group led by López Rega, who was both Perón's secretary and Isabelita's lover. Had the stakes not been so enormously high, it might have sounded like one more tango drama.

After Perón's death in July 1974, Isabelita assumed the presidency. Corruption was rife and, more importantly, López Rega launched a savage assault against the Left of the Peronist movement, organizing groups of thugs to attack trade union and political activists and passing legislation that increasingly limited or forbade oppositional activity. A massive strike in the town of Villa Constitución early in 1975 proved to be a crucial test of strength between government and the social movement. The government's response was to introduce severe austerity measures which provoked a national general strike in July. As López Rega pursued his systematic persecution of the Left under the guise of an anti-terrorist campaign mounted by the military, the war between the two wings of Peronism became in reasingly bitter and violent. The economy, meanwhile, was spiralling into crisis, and the open relationships between the Argentine military and the newly established military dictatorships in neighbouring Chile and Uruguay were a chilling warning of what was to come.

In fact, the Argentine military were themselves actively preparing a coup – there was only disagreement over timing. In January 1976, Isabelita had removed the final remnants of the old Peronist establishment from government, replacing them with the López Rega circle of death squads and corrupt functionaries. The reaction in the streets was instant. The coup, when it came, seemed almost inevitable. The exhausting struggles of previous months involved tens of thousands of working-class people; but in the end they found themselves battling against their own erstwhile leaders. By the time the military seized power in March 1976, a demoralized trade union movement seemed unable to maintain the resistance any longer.

The military regime led by Jorge Videla now embarked on
a process of political repression that gave the world the word
'disappeared' as an active verb meaning the kidnapping, torture
and murder of political opponents. 'The Dirty War' which was
immediately set in motion was a systematic campaign designed
to root out a generation of socialists and working-class militants.
Its true dimensions only emerged after the fall of the military in
1983, when the names of its thousands of victims, adults and children
began to be published. Yet even while it was in progress, the
courageous women of the Plaza de Mayo began their Thursday
morning demonstrations in front of the presidential palace,
demanding to know the whereabouts of their 'disappeared'
relatives. Their white scarves became global symbols of the
fight for human rights.[1]

For political opponents, Argentine society became a place of
fear and silence. Ford Falcons without number plates cruised the
streets with their cargo of secret police, kidnapping and disappearing anyone suspected of opposing the regime. Their victims
would join the lists of the disappeared and later their children,
some born in the secret prisons, would discover that they were
not the sons and daughters of the military or police families with
whom they lived.

For those threatened by repression who had the opportunity
to escape, the alternative was exile. The ideology of the new
government, like the conservative regimes before it, was overtly
racist, anti-Semitic and of course anti-communist. Musicians and
artists had played an important role in the earlier movements of
resistance. The Latin American protest song movement had outstanding Argentine representatives in Mercedes Sosa, Léon Gieco
and others. In Uruguay, a parallel and equally brutal repression
had begun in 1974, and there too musicians, like Daniel Viglietti
and Alfredo Zitarrosa, were forced to sing from exile. Argentina's
rock nacional, led by musicians like Charly García, enjoyed the

enthusiastic support of urban youth. Tango, now dominated by
the tango nuevo of Piazzolla and others, maintained its small local
audiences, though it was gaining a following in Europe. Tango
had proved time and again that reports of its death or disappearance
were premature.

Fernando Solanas was a key figure in the vigorous and diverse
world of Argentine cinema.[2] His iconic film *La hora de los hornos*
(The Hour of the Furnaces) was radical in every sense, politically
and aesthetically. Released in 1969, it exemplified what Solanas
himself described as a 'third cinema':[3] radical in content – it was
shaped by Peronist ideas – it was cinema as a political instrument,
a means of agitation. It was banned by the existing regime, but
shown in factories and schools; this method of distribution was
made easier by its episodic structure and its deliberately roughcast
style. But its fierce critique of neocolonialism and its creative use
of montage gave artistic form to the ideology of resistance.

Clearly, Solanas would appear on the list of those pursued by
the military and he moved to France to join the community of
Latin American political exiles in the French capital. There he
made what is arguably his most complex and most important film,
El Exilio de Gardel (Tangos), eventually issued in 1984. The film's
theme is, at its simplest, exile and its impact on individuals and
communities. A community of Argentines exiled in Paris are
preparing a tango show. The film opens with a couple on a bridge
across the Seine dancing a stylized and balletic version of tango –
its artistic and Europeanized expression. But when the couple move
down beneath the bridge and dance their tango on the towpath, it
is the recognizable, erotic encounter of tango's origins. It is perhaps
the moment of rediscovery of Argentina, of the community idealized in the tango-song bound together by its sense of marginality; an
interior exile nostalgic in its turn for another half-remembered place.

But it is also a sensual encounter. Later we meet the members
of the ensemble on a rooftop, responding like automata to

electronic sounds, until those sounds merge with the music of Piazzolla which awakens and rehumanizes the characters.

In this complex film the sensual utopia of tango is inter-woven with the shocking memories of the military regime, of the disappeared and the raw relived experiences of torture and imprisonment. Begun in 1981, it was completed just as the military regime fell in the wake of the war with Britain over the Malvinas, to be replaced (in 1984) by a return to democracy. But it was a return against a background of rage and distress and of gathering economic crisis. The film was not well received at first; tango seemed to some to belong to a world that had been murdered by the Dirty War, and to be too oblique and symbolic for a society that now expected its film and theatre to unmask the period of government terror.

Yet *El Exilio de Gardel (Tangos)* did address important and complex issues of national identity and community in the aftermath of a period that had torn apart the notion of a shared culture. Solanas's exploration of tango and its rediscovery of Gardel and Discépolo as the icons of its Golden Age are essentially journeys through the consciousness of exile, its references, its nostalgia, its preservation of a national imaginary. His subsequent film, with its soundtrack also by Piazzolla, addressed the opposite phenomenon, defined by Uruguayan writer Mario Benedetti as 'el desexilio' – 'dis-exile', or more conventionally, the return from exile.

> Nostalgia is often a feature of exile, but counter-nostalgia may equally be a feature of the return from exile. Just as the home country is not a flag or an anthem, but the sum of our child-hoods, our skies, our friends, our teachers, our loves, our streets, our kitchens, our songs, our books, our language and our sun, the country that takes us in gives us its own fervour, hatreds, habits, words, gestures, landscapes, rebellions and

there comes a moment when we become a curious conjuncture of different cultures and dreams . . .[4]

The film was *Sur*. Its protagonist, Floreal, is a trade unionist imprisoned by the regime, who, on his release, wanders the streets of Buenos Aires through a long night, afraid of returning to his home and his wife. In this case, it was the loss of his own landscape rather than the acquisition of another which produced his alienation from his own world. His nocturnal conversations with El Negro, a murdered ex-comrade, lead him finally to reconciliation and return to his broken society with the dawn.

The iconic tango 'Vuelvo al sur' (I return to the south), with music by Piazzolla and words by Solanas himself, accompanies the protagonist through this nocturnal journey into his own soul. But he returns, as you always do, to what is most familiar and most welcoming, with doubts, fears and confusions, but with love. Piazzolla's bandoneon illustrates the drama and inner conflict that attend the journey, but its sound itself is in a way what draws Floreal inexorably back. Solanas himself subsequently turned to politics, and is currently a member of the Argentine Senate.

The irony of all this is that, not for the first time, the revival of tango in Argentina itself began in Paris, or at least in Europe. After the defeat of the military government, the exiles began to return; but in the interim many of Argentina's finest tango artists – musicians, singers, dancers – had also left Argentina, sometimes for political reasons, sometimes because the decline of tango had left them with few means of earning a living. Some of the old dance ensembles had survived in the salons that remained open for their largely ageing clientele. The resurgent nationalism of a younger generation found its favoured expression in contemporary rock music or in the music of a protest song movement which embraced the whole of Latin America and part of which brought a rediscovery of national folk traditions in the music of Jorge Cafrune, Atahualpa Yupanqui or Léon Gieco.

Those tango musicians who had survived were largely of the old New Guard, dedicated to keeping alive the Golden Age of tango and to dance. Radio probably contributed more than anything else to maintaining enthusiasm for tango, at least among its devotees, but radio itself was highly territorial and it was unlikely that new younger audiences would be drawn to what felt like an exercise in nostalgia.

Europe, by contrast, was discovering tango anew in a theatrical context. The towering success of the show *Tango Argentino* at its first showing in Paris in 1983 was not easy to predict. The show was ten years in the making and its performers were not in their first flush of youth; great dancers though they were, Juan Carlos Copes and Virulazo were no longer young, and nor was Roberto Goyeneche, the acclaimed tango singer. According to the show's director, Claudio Segovia, only 250 tickets had been sold days before the performance in Paris in a 2,500-seater theatre. Yet, on the day, it was a runaway success and set a precedent for a series of identical shows to follow. *Tango Argentino* sold out wherever it was produced, and has continued to do so for twenty years around the world – though the great breakthrough was probably its sell-out shows on Broadway.

We could speculate endlessly on the reasons for the acclaim it enjoyed and continues to enjoy. The precedent, of course, was Piazzolla, who had won a growing and appreciative audience for his 'tango nuevo'. Jazz and classical musicians like Gary Burton and the Kronos Quartet performed with him and his compositions became a standard part of their repertoire. But outside Latin America the dance still belonged to the ballroom dancers in the bowdlerized version that owed more to the manuals of Vernon and Irene Castle at the beginning of the century than to the sensual dramas played out by dancers like El Cachafaz in the same era.

Street tango in Buenos Aires.

Tango Argentino, by contrast, was athletic, sensual and balletic – it was modern dance with interwoven bodies and an open sexual interplay. And it was a dramatic and beautiful spectacle. Its scenario was nostalgic and evocative of an underworld whose vocabulary and characters were widely recognizable – though not necessarily as Argentine. Perhaps its success was that it made seduction, hetero-sexual and homoerotic, acceptable not just on stage, but in the intimacy of the dance salon. Yet its impact was most problematic in Argentina itself – at least at first. Claudio Segovia reports that it was difficult to win an audience and the show was not presented there until nearly a decade later. Perhaps it was once again the case that it was Europe's enthusiasm for tango that regenerated interest in its homeland. But it is also true that a new phenomenon, *tango nuevo*, a new musical fusion, built around the work of Piazzolla (who died in 1992), was winning back the young to tango in electronic versions by groups like the Gotan Project or Bajofondo Tango Club.

Today, Buenos Aires has rediscovered tango as a language that connects it with a wider world. It is the source of a good part of its tourist income. In 2010, it was recognized by UNESCO as part of 'the intangible cultural heritage of humankind'. In late 2011, a demonstration at the Retiro Station demanded that the government devote more resources to its preservation. In China, it has become a form of protest against government repression.

Tango's extraordinary resilience tells a story beyond survival; it is a demonstration that its music and poetry respond to a deep sensual desire in all of us.

TANGO IN THE WORLD

In fact, tango had led a double life for many years. The ups and downs of its acceptance in Argentina were matched, but not exactly paralleled by its fate elsewhere – and sometimes in places that would seem to have very little in common with the society that gave the tango birth.

Tango was brought to Finland by a Danish couple who danced it at the Börs Hotel in Helsinki in 1913. Odeon Records (founded in Berlin in 1903) was aggressively exporting its catalogue across Europe as well as to the United States and it continued to do so until 1936 when the Nazi government appointed a new, politically reliable director who substituted acceptable 'Aryan' recordings for the broad range of ethnic musics offered by Odeon. When the Argentine operation became independent during and

after the First World War, under Max Glücksmann, his new Discos
Nacional label produced a much more authentic tango sound than
its parent company whose recordings tended towards march
rhythms in slower time. Finland took its lead from the German
interpretation, and through the 1920s and 1930s Finnish tango
echoed the heavier tread of the German version. With the Second
World War, however, the ties were severed and a new Finnish
tango emerged, now described as a 'national tango', whose references and language owed more to rural traditions than to the
urban scene. Its rhythms are more languid than the Argentine
tango; its lyrics express the same yearning for love and nostalgia
for a better time as its Argentine equivalent. But the most famous
of them all, Unto Mononen's 'Satumaa' (written in 1947, but most
commercially successful in the 1960s in Reijo Tapale's recording)
creates an imaginary place outside time, a paradise, where 'the
concerns of tomorrow can be forgotten' and love waits patiently.[5]

Mononen's iconic 'Satumaa' sits more comfortably within the
tradition of a romantic ballad, and was sung for the slower and
more formal dances in Finland's outdoor summer pavilions. But
just as foreign music became the vogue for youth in the early
1960s, tango had its own revival. The star tango singer Reijo
Tapale's recording of 'Satumaa' was at the top of the record
charts in November 1961 and the same singer's 'Takdet meren
ylla' (Takdet by the sea) competed with the Beatles' 'All My Loving'
for number one in 1964. Popular among an older generation,
tango had a second rebirth in the late 1980s, when the Seinajoki
tango festival attracted crowds for the election of the Tango King
and Queen which exceeded 100,000 every year by the end of the
Nineties.

Equally surprising, perhaps, is the enormous enthusiasm for
tango in Japan. It was first introduced by an aristocrat, Baron

Modern tango dancers.

Megata, who learned tango in Paris while convalescing from an illness and opened a tango academy on his return to Tokyo in 1926. The first tango orchestra to visit Japan, however, was Juan Canaro's in 1954. A year earlier, Argentina was surprised to hear the recordings of the singer Ranko Fujisawa, who had learnt her tangos phonetically. Francisco Canaro followed in 1961, but it was in the 1970s – during tango's lean years at home – that many of Argentina's finest musicians visited Japan. It was, furthermore, a two-way traffic, with Japanese exponents of the 'new Japanese tango' visiting the salons of Buenos Aires. It was generally the dance that attracted the vast number of Japanese followers, and it was relatively late when bandoneon player Ryota Kamatsu was able to win appreciation for the Piazzolla style. In 2009, Hiroshi and Kyoko Yamao won the tango salon category at tango's world championship in Buenos Aires, El Mundial.[6]

By the 1990s, tango was danced everywhere – split skirts and high-heeled dancing shows had made a triumphant return and men in many countries were learning once again to hold their partners firmly and press their bodies into a sensual embrace. Tango show followed tango show, and tango dancers have become noticeably younger and more confidently experimental.

Significantly, given tango's origins, women have become more and more central to tango, as musicians, orchestra leaders and singers. Susana Rinaldi is just one among many of the accomplished singers of a new generation. Tango has also had its equivalent of the 'Buena Vista Social Club'. *Café de los Maestros* (Walter Salles, 2009) chronicles the concert given by the finest singers and players of tango's Golden Age at Buenos Aires Teatro Colón, from which tango had so long been excluded.

TANGO STORIES: PARTNERS

NORMA'S STORY

I was always fascinated by tango, and always intended to learn, but for different reasons I never got round to it. I went to Buenos Aires at a difficult moment in my life, and I went to a show that moved me so deeply that I decided to go to a class. I was lucky enough to find an excellent teacher here in Salta, where I live. I attended a weekly class but I was so absorbed that the wait between classes felt like an eternity; I couldn't wait for those two hours every Saturday.

Dance was always central to my life; I started ballet when I was very young and kept at it for a long time. My dream was to be a ballerina, but it just wasn't to be. I started tango five years ago and I haven't stopped dancing since then; it's my life, it entraps you. After a while, the teacher asked me to dance with him in a tango show. I couldn't believe it. Of course, I said 'yes' immediately, though inside I was very scared. I had spent so long doing other very different things that I wasn't sure I could do it. But luckily the body has its own memory, and little by little the things I had learned in all those years of classical dance came back to me. It was as if life had given me a second chance to do what I most wanted to do in life. Since then, tango has become more and more central to my life, it is my passion. It's as if there had been something missing – expressing myself with my body.

I think things changed very much with the tango festivals and championships. What began as a way of attracting tourism has become a worldwide phenomenon, with schools opening everywhere. New styles have emerged too, which have caught the interest of the young who are getting to know the history and the codes of tango. The world championships are attracting more and more people, and the city is completely full while they are on. People are so keen to see tango that there are open-air tango shows going on. And now tango has been declared a world heritage too.

We met dancing tango. He was my only teacher at first, and he still is my teacher and dance partner. But we began to realize that something else was going on. For a year now, he has been my life companion too. I would say that we came to this relationship through sharing a passion for tango, which always moves things within you, even love.

The connection of two bodies in the embrace and the perfect connection in the dance is attractive and pleasurable; tango is full of seduction.

The way you dress is important, especially when you're dancing for an audience. If you're doing a show, you have to wear attractive clothes that allow you to shine, but they have to be comfortable enough to dance in too. The split skirt is elegant and sensual and lets you move freely. And you need to be well made-up and wear the high heels that add to this elegance. I think every woman who really feels like a woman likes to be feminine and dress adds to that feeling of our own attraction.

The feminine and the masculine are both very marked in the tango; it represents the relationship between men and women. So the way you dress underlines the seduction and the desire to attract your partner.

JOSÉ'S STORY

For me, tango is life itself; from the moment I began, at nineteen, it has marked my life. I already liked the music, and I played some instruments, and then one Saturday night I saw tango on TV and I haven't stopped dancing since. I began to dance, using my body and my feet as musical instruments. Within the year, I was teaching, and I grew together with tango.

Meeting your partner means two different things. On the dance floor you nod your head to invite the woman to dance; if she accepts you, you come together in an embrace that unites two bodies with a special energy accompanied by the music, until you achieve that union of bodies that produces dreams and moments of passion. Then there is the meeting in life, where the tango is an accomplice to love, because you fall in love not just with tango but with the person who enjoys the dancing. Romance begins in tango rhythm, turning it into something necessary and sublime for continuing our life as a couple.

Tango moves so many things within you that you often abandon everything else, sometimes even giving up on other important aspects of your life, like having children or spending time on other enjoyable activities. You feel so seductive when you're dancing tango, not because you're trying to but because it's part of the tango itself. It's something you never give up on – I'm a teacher and it's my vocation to make it known across the world. And when I watch people dance, I'm proud to have added my grain of sand to the happiness of others.

When I hear the first note, I feel a warmth, an emotion course through my body, an energy is released that I share with my partner. Because the ideal partner is one you share your life with.

I've been teaching for 27 years and dancing in shows and events; my years with tango have brought me great happiness. I've shared my passion with Argentines and foreigners, which has confirmed that tango is universal and everyone can feel it.

The tango boom today begins with the rediscovery of the dance and its recognition as a couple dance. It improves your self-esteem and puts you in touch with strong feelings towards the dance and your partner. And in addition, studies have shown that tango is good for the heart. And once you start you can't stop, which means it's important to discover it at the right moment of your life.

A CYCLE OF REBIRTH

One question remains. What is it about Argentine tango that appeals to and excites such passion? Dance is surrender of the self to the body.

> At times with a new partner I have felt fear during our first dance. Can we really be this close, hearts beating together, smelling each other, sweat mingling, moving as one?[7]

Tango, then, is intimacy made doubly dramatic by the absence of words, of explanation, that precedes the invitation to the dance, and the complete absorption with the music, which inhibits talk of any kind during the three-minute encounter. Yet there is safety too – the security of an ending, the knowledge that there are unspoken rules and rituals that set out invisible frontiers. The movement of several couples around the floor is in a single direction – and there are elaborate measures to avoid collision. The basis of the meeting is trust; the woman is willing to surrender to this unnamed partner, this stranger. Why this should work as it does is still a mystery, unless it is the same impulse that allows us to assume risk and danger as the threshold of pleasure. Because for both partners that risk is present, even if the history of the dance, its origins and gestures, emerge from a world of dominant males, the tango tells us in a hundred stories that his confidence too is fragile and evidence not only of control, but also of the lack of it in a wider world.

In a post-feminist world, these relationships are not what they seem. The ritual is maintained, though women can and do now propose as well as receive.

Yet, in many ways, the tango's past is always present. The tango, even the more romantic and dramatic tango-salon, is about sex, not love; a rehearsal of sexual passion in the brushing of legs and the swaying of the body. And yet, for the Argentine writer Ernesto Sábato, it expresses a kind of nostalgia for love and tenderness that cannot be found in casual sexual encounters, though machismo demands that the sadness is buried in a challenging masculinity. For him, it is the reflection of a national history 'dominated by maladjustment, nostalgia, sadness, frustration, dramatic experiences, discontent, resentment and other problems'.[8] The conclusion would seem to be, as Archetti suggests, that 'the tango can be seen as a discourse on human suffering and the negation of real and sincere happiness for both man and woman'.[9] One of the few tangos written by a woman (using a pseudonym, of course) seems to agree.

> *Se va la vida . . .*
> *se va y no vuelve.*
> *Escuchá este consejo;*
> *si un bacán te promete acomodar,*
> *entrá derecho viejo.*
> *Se va, pebeta,*
> *quién la detiene*
> *si ni Dios la sujeta,*
> *lo mejor es gozarla y largar*
> *las penas a rodar.*
>
> *Yo quiero,*
> *muchacha,*
> *que al fin mostrés la hilacha*
> *y al mishio*
> *recuerdo*
> *le des un golpe de hacha.*
> *Decí, pa qué queres*
> *llorar un amor*
> *y morir, tal vez,*
> *de desesperanza.*
> *No rogués la flor*

de un sueño infeliz
porque, a lo mejor,
la suerte te alcanza
si te decidís.

Se va la vida . . .
se va y no vuelve,
escuchá este consejo;
si un bacán te promete acomodar,
entrá derecho viejo.
Pasan los días,
pasan los años,
es fugaz la alegría,
no pensés en dolor ni en virtud,
viví tu juventud.

Life fades away / and never returns / Here's my advice / if a rich
man promises to look after you / get in there. / Life passes, girl /
no stopping it / not even God can stop it / so the best thing to do
is enjoy it and send / sorrows on their way.
Girl / I want you / to show some backbone / and kick the memory
of poverty / into the ditch. / Tell me / why cry over a lover / and
die maybe / of despair? / Don't chase / an unhappy dream /
because fate might / catch up with you / if you make a decision.
Life fades away / and never returns / Here's my advice / if a rich
man promises to look after you / get in there. / The days pass /
years pass / happiness is fleeting / don't think of pain or virtue /
live your youth while you have it.
      ('Se va la vida', Life passes you by – María Luisa Carnelli, 1929)

Yet the repeated resurgence of tango across the world suggests a
different reading. The boom of recent decades is above all a dance
boom, though the settings of the theatrical representations

insistently return to the demi-monde of prostitutes, pimps and red-light districts. Some have described this as a new variety of *nostalgie de la boue*, a fascination with the transgressive, the forbidden world of sexual experiment and perversion. Like the *milonguera*, the tango dancers of the present enter the three-minute contract willingly, abandoning the complex negotiations that govern the physical encounters between genders of which feminism has taught us to be constantly aware. Life, after all, soon passes.

CHRONOLOGY

1536

First settlement at Buenos Aires established by Pedro de Mendoza.

1541

Buenos Aires abandoned after Indian attacks.

1580

A second settlement of Buenos Aires established by Juan de Garay.

1609

Jesuit Missions founded in the Upper Paraná.

1620

Buenos Aires becomes capital of the province of the same name.

1767

Jesuits expelled from all Spanish territories.

1776

Viceroyalty of Rio de la Plata established as a separate region and the port of Buenos Aires begins to flourish with the export of goods like leather.

1806–7

British attempts to occupy Buenos Aires.

1810

The May revolution deposes the Spanish viceroy, and the process of Argentine independence begins. These events are a response to the Napoleonic invasion of Spain.

1816

The Argentine Declaration of Independence issued by the Congress of Tucuman.

1820

The Battle of Cepeda is the first military confrontation between Federalists and Centralists.

1826

Bernardino Rivadavia named first President of Argentina, but the provinces refuse to accept his nomination and he resigns.

1828

Independence of Uruguay.

1829–3

The first rule of Juan Manuel de Rosas (the model for Sarmiento's *Facundo*).

1833

British forces re-occupy the Falkland Islands / Malvinas.

1835

Rosas's second period of rule begins.

1838–40

French blockade of the River Plate.

1839

Rosas made Supreme Leader of the Argentine Confederation.

1845–9

French and British blockade the River Plate.

1845

Sarmiento's *Facundo* is published.
Rosas overthrown by Urquiza. Yellow fever epidemic in Buenos Aires.

1853

Constitution of Argentina passed under the presidency of Urquiza. Buenos Aires refuses to accept it and secedes to become the State of Buenos Aires.

1857

Teatro Colón opens.

1858

Café Tortoni opens for business. New yellow fever epidemic in Buenos Aires

1859

Unitarian forces under Bartolome Mitre are defeated at the second Battle of Cepeda by Urquiza's federal forces.

1862

Buenos Aires rejoins the federation and Bartolome Mitre is elected the first president of a unified country.

1864–70

War of the Triple Alliance.

1865

Constitución railway station opened.

1867

Cholera epidemic in Buenos Aires.

1868

Birth of Angel Villoldo (he dies in 1919). Rosendo Mendizábal born (he dies in 1913).

1870–71

New yellow fever outbreak in Buenos Aires.

1872

Jose Hernández publishes the first part of his epic poem *Martín Fierro*, 'La Ida'.

1878

Julio Argentino Roca launches his war against the Indians, known as the Conquest of the Desert.

1879

Publication of the second part of *Martín Fierro*, 'La Vuelta'. El Cachafaz (José Ovidio Banquet), most famous of early tango dancers, born (he dies in 1942).

1880

Roca becomes president and Buenos Aires becomes the official capital. The beginning of the Guardia Vieja, whose dominion over tango would last until around 1917.

1888

'Dame la lata', regarded as the first tango with lyrics, is performed. Pascual Contursi born (he dies in 1932).

1890

Carlos Gardel born in Toulouse, France.

1894

Construction of Avenida de Mayo completed.

1895

Museo de Bellas Artes (Fine Arts Museum) opens in Buenos Aires.

1896

Rosita Quiroga born (she dies in 1984).

1897

Rosendo Mendizábal composes 'El entrerriano'.

1898

Caras y caretas the magazine which gave extensive coverage to early tango, is founded.

1900

Juan D'Arienzo, 'the king of rhythm', born (he dies in 1976).

1902

Azucena Maizani born (he dies in 1970).

1903

Angel Villoldo's 'El Choclo' released. The Casa Rosada, the presidential palace, is built. Election of José Batlle to the Uruguayan presidency.

1904

Mercedes Simone born (he dies in 1990). Sofia Bazan born (dies in 1958). Tita Merello born (dies in 2002).

1905

Francisco Fiorentino born (he dies in 1955). Osvaldo Pugliese born (dies in 1995).

1907

Rent strike in the *conventillos*.

1908

Teatro Colon opened. Atahualpa Yupanqui born (he dies in 1992).

1911

Publication of Ricardo Guiraldes's poem 'Tango'.

1912

Roque Saenz Peña's government introduces universal suffrage and the secret ballot. Baron Antonio de Marchi organizes his tango night at the Palais de Glace, Buenos Aires. The musical *The Sunshine Girl* opens in London.

1913

Buenos Aires underground starts operation. Richepin's *Le Tango* opens in Paris.

1914

Birth of Anibal Troilo, 'Pichuco' (he dies in 1975).

1916

Hipolito Yrigoyen elected to the presidency. Buenos Aires Stock Exchange built.

1917

First performance of Pascual Contursi's 'Mi noche triste' performed and recorded by Carlos Gardel in the same year. Tango 'La Cumparsita', by Uruguayan Gerardo Matos Rodríguez, performed for first time.

1918

The University Reform movement in Córdoba transforms the university there.

1919

La Semana Trágica, the Tragic Week, in which several hundred people are killed in clashes between striking workers and right-wing strike breakers.

1921

The Four Horsemen of the Apocalypse released. Birth of Astor Piazzola (he dies in 1992)

1926

Roberto Goyeneche born (he dies in 1994). Julio Sosa born (dies in 1964).

1928–30

Second administration of Hipolito Yrigoyen.

1929

Birth of Ernesto 'Che' Guevara.

1930

Irigoyen is overthrown in a military coup and replaced by a military government headed by Jose Feliz Uruburu.

1931

Luces de Buenos Aires, directed by Adelqui Millar, and starring Carlos Gardel, is released.

1933

¡Tango! (dir Moglia Barth) the first Argentina sound film, released.

1934

Tango en Broadway, directed by Louis Garnier and starring Gardel, released.

1935

Death in an air accident of Carlos Gardel and Alfredo Le Pera. *Tango Bar* (dir. John Reinhardt) released. *El día que me quieras* (dir. John Reinhardt) released. Birth of Susana Rinaldi.

1937

Avenida 9 de Julio opened. Jorge Cafrune born (he dies in 1978).

1943

The so-called 'national revolution' brings in a military government that includes Colonel Juan Perón as Minister of Labour.

1945

March: Argentina enters World War Two on the side of the Allies. Perón arrested and then freed in the face of popular protests.

1946

Perón elected to the Presidency.

1951

Perón's second presidential term.

1952

Death of Evita Perón.

1955

Perón ousted by the so-called 'Liberating Revolution'.

1962

Government led by Arturo Frondizi overthrown in military coup. Academia Porteña del Lunfardo founded.

1964

Mrozek's 'Tango' performed for the first time.

1966

Juan Carlos de Onganía assumes power and bans political parties.

1967

Astor Piazzola begins his collaboration with Horacio Ferrer.

1968

Release of *La hora de los hornos* (The hour of the furnaces) directed by Solanas and Getino.

1969

'Balada para un loco' by Piazzola and Ferrer released.

1970

Alejandro Lanusse replaces Ongania.

1972

Last Tango in Paris, directed by Bernardo Bertolucci, is a *succès de scandale*.

1973

Perón returns from exile. Members of the extreme right-wing Triple A (Argentine Anticommunist Alliance) open fire on the crowds awaiting him outside Ezeiza airport. Héctor Cámpora elected as a caretaker candidate to the presidency. Perón elected later that year. The civilian-military regime in Uruguay suspends civil rights and imposes an military dictatorship under Bordaberry.

1974

Perón dies, leaving his second wife, María Isabel, to assume the presidency.

1976

Military coup deposes Peronist government, and Jorge Videla heads the military government. It launches repression across the country, with the extensive use of torture and state assassination. This 'Dirty War' continues until 1983.

1977

Demonstrations by the Mothers of the Plaza de Mayo begin in which relatives of people 'disappeared' by the military regime demand to know their whereabouts and their fate.

1978

Argentina hosts and wins the soccer World Cup.

1982

Argentine troops sent to the Falkland Islands / Malvinas. The islands are retaken by British troops later that year.

1983

Collapse of Galtieri regime. Raul Alfonsín elected to the presidency. The show *Tango Argentino* opens in Paris to become a huge international success.

1985

La historia oficial (The official version) wins Academy Award for best foreign film. *El exilio de Gardel (Tangos)*, directed by Fernando Solanas, released.

1988

'Tango ×2', a tribute to Gardel begins its extensive tour of Latin America and Europe. *Sur*, directed by Fernando Solanas, released.

1989

Peronist Carlos Menem elected to the presidency. He is re-elected in 1995.

1990

National Academy of the Tango founded.

1993

Tango, directed by Patrice Leconte, is released.

2001

Argentinazo – widespread protests at economic chaos and retaliatory measures by IMF and World Bank across the country.

2003

Peronist Néstor Kirchner wins presidency.

2007

Cristina Kirchner assumes presidency.

2009

Walter Salles's *El café de los maestros* released.

REFERENCES

1 STRANGERS IN THE CITY

1 Richard J. Watter, *Politics and Urban Growth in Buenos Aires, 1910–1942* (Cambridge, 1993), p. 6.
2 See David Rock, *Argentina, 1516–1987* (Berkeley, CA, 1987).
3 D. F. Sarmiento, *Facundo: Civilization and Barbarism*, trans. Kathleen Ross (Berkeley, CA, 2003).
4 See Peter H. Smith, *Politics and Beef in Argentina: Patterns of Conflict and Change* (New York, 1969).
5 On the war of the Triple Alliance, see Chris Leuchars, *To the Bitter End: Paraguay and the War of the Triple Alliance* (Westport, CT, 2002).
6 See Rock, *Argentina*, pp. 133–6.
7 J. Hernández, *Martin Fierro*. An English translation, less liberal than mine, can be found at: http://sparrowthorn.com.
8 Quoted in Donna J. Guy, *Sex and Danger in Buenos Aires: Prostitution, Family and Nation in Argentina* (Lincoln, NE, 1991), p. 10.
9 German García, *El inmigrante en la novela argentina* (Buenos Aires, 1970), p. 52.
10 See Karin Grammático, 'Obreras, prostitutas y mal venéreo. Un Estado ern busca de la profilaxis', in *Historia de las mujeres en la Argentina Siglo* xx, ed. Fernanda Gil Lozano, Valeria Silvina Pita and María Gabriel Ini (Buenos Aires, 2000), pp. 117–36.
11 Jo Baim, 'The Tango: Icon of Culture, Music, and Dance in Argentina, Europe and the United States from 1875 to 1925', PhD thesis, University of Oregon, 1997, p. 1. See Jo Baim, *Tango: Creation of a Cultural Icon* (Bloomington, IN, 2007).
12 Marta E. Savigliano, *Tango and the Political Economy of Passion* (Boulder, CO, 1995), pp. xiv–xv.
13 Julie Taylor, 'Tango: Theme of Class and Nation' in *Ethnomusicology*, xx/2 (May 1976), p. 276.
14 Ibid.

2 A CITY DIVIDED

1 See David T. Keeling, *Buenos Aires: Global Dreams, Local Crises* (Chichester, 1996).
2 David Rock, *Argentina, 1516–1987* (Berkeley, CA, 1987), p. 132.
3 Chris Moss, *Patagonia: A Cultural History* (New York, 2008). See also Bruce Chatwin, *In Patagonia* (New York, 1977).
4 Walter Benjamin, 'Paris, Capital of the Nineteenth Century', in *The Arcades Project* (Cambridge, MA, and London, 1999) pp. 14–26.
5 Mempo Giardinelli, *Santo oficio de la memoria* (Barcelona, 1997).
6 For example, E. Cambácres, *Sin rumbo* (Lajouane, Buenos Aires, 1885).
7 Marta E. Savigliano, *Tango and the Political Economy of Passion* (Boulder, CO, 1995), p. 47.
8 Jo Baim, 'The Tango: Icon of Culture, Music, and Dance in Argentina, Europe and the United States from 1875 to 1925', PhD thesis, University of Oregon, 1997, p. 38.
9 Julie Taylor, *Paper Tangos* (Durham, NC, 2003), p. 11.
10 Goyo Cuello quoted in Jo Baim, *The Tango*, p. 47.
11 Quoted in Savigliano, *Tango and the Political Economy*, p. 115.
12 Keeling, *Buenos Aires*, p. 229.

3 TANGO GOES TO PARIS

1 Walter Benjamin, 'Paris, Capital of the Nineteenth Century', in *The Arcades Project* (Cambridge, MA, and London, 1999), pp. 14–26.
2 Nicholas Hewitt, 'Shifting Cultural Centres in Twentieth-century Paris', in *Parisian Fields*, ed. Michael Sheringham (London, 1997), p. 33.
3 See Alexander C. T. Goeppert, *Fleeting Cities: Imperial Expositions in Fin-de-Siècle Europe* (Basingstoke and New York, 2010).
4 See C. M. Brosteanu, 'The influence of the exotic in early erotic photography' at www.brosteanu.com/erotic-photograph/2010 (accessed 12 June 2012).
5 See Richard Powers, 'The hidden story of the Apache dance' at http://socialdance.stanford.edu/syllabi/Apache1.htm (accessed 10 June 2012). YouTube also has a large selection of short films showing the dance.
6 Blas Matamoro, *El Tango* (Madrid, 1997), p. 25.
7 'Paris', at www.Tango%20Libre.webarchive (accessed 12 May 2012).
8 Salaverria, quoted in M. Savigliano, *Tango and the Political Economy of Passion* (Boulder, CO, 1995), pp. 115–16.

9   Matamoro, *El Tango*, p. 26.
10 R. Guiraldes, 'Tango', in *El cencerro de cristal* (Buenos Aires, 1915).
11 R. Guiraldes, *Don Segundo Sombra* (San Antonio de Areco, 1926).
12 Jean Cocteau, *Le passé defini*, quoted in Matamoro, *El Tango*, p. 27.
13 Jo Baim, *Tango: Creation of a Cultural Icon* (Bloomington, IN, 2007), pp. 60–67. Baim also notes the large number of articles about tango published in the U.S. in the following three years.
14 Quoted in Baim, *Tango: Creation*, p. 76.
15 Ibid.
16 Savigliano, *Tango*, p. 47.
17 Julie Verbert, 'The tango dancer's costume' at www.alterinfos.org/spip.php?rubrique159 (accessed 13 March 2012).
18 R. Cunninghame Graham, *Rodeo: A Collection of the Tales and Sketches of R. B. Cunninghame Graham* (Whitefish, MT, 2005), pp. 133–4.
19 Matamoro, *El Tango*, pp. 26–7.
20 Savigliano, *Tango*, p. 117.
21 Ibid., p. 119.
22 Quoted in John Storm Roberts, *The Latin Tinge* (New York, 1999), p. 46.
23 Halsey K. Mohr, 'The Tango in the Sky', quoted in Baim, *Tango: Creation*, p. 13.
24 Roberts, *The Latin Tinge*, pp. 48–9.
25 Savigliano, *Tango*, pp. 147–8.
26 Matamoro, *El Tango*, p. 31.
27 Savigliano, *Tango*, p. 138.

4 TANGO FINDS ITS VOICE

1   David Rock, *Politics in Argentina, 1890–1930: The Rise and Fall of Radicalism* (Cambridge, 1975) pp. 32–3.
2   Ibid., p. 50.
3   Richard J. Walter, *Politics and Urban Growth in Buenos Aires, 1910–1942* (Cambridge, 1993), chap. 3.
4   Paul Vernon, 'The Tango Trip' in *Folk Roots* (2004), pp. 33–4.
5   Donna Guy, *Sex and Danger in Buenos Aires: Prostitution, Family and Nation in Argentina* (Lincoln, NE, 1995), p. 33.
6   The phrase is Julio Mafud's in *Sociología del tango* (Buenos Aires, 1965).

8   Julie Taylor, *Paper Tangos* (Durham, NC, and London, 2003), p. 11.
9   See F. Gil Lozano et al., eds, *Historia de las mujeres en la Argentina, Siglo XX* (Buenos Aires, 2000), pp. 197–223.

10 See Walter Benjamin, 'On Some Motifs in Baudelaire', in *Illuminations*, trans. Harry Zohn (London, 1970), pp.157–202.

5 GARDEL AND THE GOLDEN AGE

1 See Pablo Antonio Paranagua, *Mexican Cinema* (London, 1996).
2 See Simon Collier, *The Life, Music and Times of Carlos Gardel* (Pittsburgh, PA, 1986).
3 See Simon Collier 'Carlos Gardel and the Cinema' at www.gardelweb.com (accessed 13 April 2012).
4 José Ignacio Cabrujas, *El día que me quieras* (Caracas, 1997), p. 24.
5 See George Dangerfield, *The Strange Death of Liberal England* (London, 1935).
6 Sung with passion and intensity in a recent incarnation by Estrella Morente in Pedro Almodóvar's film of the same name.
7 Ed Archetti, *Masculinities: Football, Polo and the Tango in Argentina* (Berlin, 1989), p. 149.
8 Ernesto Sábato quoted in Julie Taylor, 'Tango: Theme of Class and Nation', in *Ethnomusicology*, xx/2 (May 1976), p. 277.
9 Donald S. Castro, 'Popular Culture as a Source for Historians: The Tango in its Epoca de Oro, 1917–1943', in *Journal of Popular Culture*, xxix/3 (Winter, 1986), p. 47.

6 THE DYING OF THE LIGHT

1 See N. Torrents and John King, *The Garden of Forking Paths: Argentine Cinema* (London, 1988). See also Matamoro, *El Tango*, pp. 76–7.
2 See chapter 5.
3 See Matamoro, *El Tango*, pp. 74–8.
4 Simon Collier et al., *¡Tango!, the Dance, the Song, the Story* (London, 1995), p. 153. This volume contains some extraordinary photographs of the crowded dance halls of the period (on p. 155, for example).
5 Matamoro, *El Tango*, p. 83.
6 Ibid., p. 85.
7 Legend has it that the song was in fact deeply personal, commemorating Contursi's lifelong unconsummated fascination with the singer Susana Grisel.
8 Tomas Eloy Martinez's *Santa Evita* (London, 1997) explores the myth beautifully. And Tim Rice and Andrew Lloyd Webber's *Evita* brought her image to an even wider audience.

9 Rock, *Politics in Argentina*, p. 239.
10 Daniel James has sensitively explored the history and power of Peronism in *Resistance and Integration: Peronism and the Argentine Working Class, 1946–1979* (Cambridge, 1988), and the excellent *Doña María's Story: Life, History, Memory and Political Identity* (Durham, NC, 2000).
11 James, *Resistance and Integration*, p. 290.

7 ASTOR PIAZZOLA AND TANGO NUEVO

1 Evita's charitable foundation collected money for earthquake victims, for example, and publicly encouraged the ladies of the upper classes to contribute their jewellery. Contemporary news footage shows that they did so, but with gritted teeth.
2 See Ronaldo Munck, *Argentina: From Anarchism to Peronism* (London, 1987), pp. 127–46.
3 For discussion of the complex politics of Peronism, see Daniel James, *Resistance and Integration: Peronism and the Argentine Working Class, 1946–1979* (Cambridge, 1988), Munck, *Argentina*, and the three-volume study by Felix Luna, *Perón y su tiempo* (Buenos Aires, 1990).
4 See Munck, *Argentina*, pp. 142–149.
5 The film *The Hour of the Furnaces* (dir. Getino and Solanas, 1968) both represents and depicts this period.
6 Munck, *Argentina*, pp. 160–61.
7 See Pablo Vila, 'Tango to Folk: Hegemony Construction and Popular Identities in Argentina', *Studies in Latin American Popular Culture*, XXIV (2005), pp. 107–39.
8 Vila, 'Tango to Folk', p. 128.
9 See María Susana Azzi and Simon Collier, *Le Grand Tango: The Life and Music of Astor Piazzolla* (Oxford, 2000). See, too, the website piazzolla.org.
10 Azzi and Collier, *Le Grand Tango*, pp. 58–9.
11 Ibid., p. 59.
12 There are a number of recordings of his performances accessible via YouTube.
13 Their collaboration is recorded, and Ferrer's poems reproduced in the two-volume *Los tangos de Ferrer y Piazzolla* (Buenos Aires, 2000) and in Horacio Ferrer's own prolific writing about tango.
14 *Los tangos de Ferrer y Piazzolla*, vol. II, p. 42.
15 Recorded and used by many people since, and differing as widely as the post-modernist disco 'queen', Grace Jones, and the fine, classical cellist and great admirer of Piazzolla, Yo-Yo Ma.

16 We will address the extraordinary impact of this show and its repercussions in chapter Eight.

8 THE LONG ROAD HOME

1 On the families of the disappeared, the film *The Official Story* (1984) and *La Cautiva* (2011) are examples. See the www.madres.org and Marguerite Guzman Bouvard, *Revolutionising Motherhood: The Mothers of the Plaza de Mayo (Latin American Silhouettes)* (Wilmington, DE, 1994).

2 See John King and Nissa Torrents, *The Garden of Forking Paths: Argentine Cinema* (London, 1996).

3 See Zuzana M. Pick, *The New Latin America Cinema: A Continental Project* (Austin, TX, 1996), pp. 167–76.

4 Mario Benedetti, 'El desexilio', in *El País* [Madrid], 18 April 1983. It is republished as the prologue to M. Benedetti, *El desexilio y otras conjeturas* (Barcelona, 1986).

5 Thanks to Riikka Gonzalez for her help. See, too, Jutta Jaakkola (2000) on the website of the Finnish Music Information Centre: www.fimic.fi.

6 See Arcángel Pascual Vardaro's very useful and well-informed *El tango en la década del 50 y otras cosas más* (Desert Hot Springs, CA, 2011). Vardaro also points out the negative consequences of Japanese tango enthusiasm: people have bought and taken so many bandoneons that few remain in Argentina, and that the Japanese remastering of old record collections return in CD form but at very high prices.

7 Claire Spooner, 'Explorations in Intimacy', *Therapy Today*, XXII/2 (March 2011), p. 18.

8 Ernesto Sábato, *Tango discusión y clave* (Buenos Aires, 1963), p. 19. Quote in Eduardo Archetti, *Masculinities* (Berlin, 1989), p. 143.

9 Archetti, *Masculinities*, p. 149.

SELECT BIBLIOGRAPHY

This list is a selection, nothing more. There are many books on tango, many of them very recent, though very often devoted to the dance alone. There are also a huge number of websites devoted to tango, but by far the most comprehensive is: www.todotango.com.

Azzi, María Susana, *Antropología del Tango – Los Protagonistas* (Buenos Aires, 1991)
—, and Simon Collier, *Le Grand Tango: The Life and Music of Astor Piazzolla* (Oxford, 2000)
Castro, Donald S., *The Argentine Tango as Social History, 1890–1955: The Soul of the People* (New York, 1991)
Chichelnitsky M. and Omar Tambasco, *Antología de letras de tango* (Barcelona, 1999)
Collier, Simon, *The Life, Music and Times of Carlos Gardel* (Pittsburgh, PA, 1986)
——, Artemis Cooper, María Susana Azzi and Richard Martin, *¡Tango!* (London, 1995)
Cunninghame, Graham, R., *Rodeo: A Collection of Tales and Sketches* (New York, 1936)
Deluy, H. and S. Yurkievich, *Le Tango* (Paris, 1988)
Denniston, Christine, *The Meaning of Tango: The Story of the Argentinian Dance* (London, 2007)
Ferrer, Horacio, *El tango: su historia y evolución* (Buenos Aires, 1964)
——, *El libro del tango: crónica y diccionario, 1850–1977* (Buenos Aires, 1980)
——, *El siglo de oro del tango* (Buenos Aires, 1996)
Flores, Rafael, 'No me lloren, crezcan: Carlos Gardel, centenario y tango inacabable' in *Cuadernos Hispanomericanos*, XLVII/91 (1990), pp. 7–28
Foster, D. W., *Imagination Beyond Nation* (Pittsburgh, PA, 1998)
Gil, Lozano, F., Valeria Silvina Pita and María Gabriela Ini, eds, *Historia de las mujeres en Argentina* (Buenos Aires, 2000)
Gobello, José, *Crónica general del tango* (Buenos Aires, 1998)

——, *Nuevo diccionario lunfardo:* Buenos Aires, 1990

Gorín, Natalio, ed., *Astor Piazzolla: a manera de memorias* (Buenos Aires, 1990)

Guy, Donna, J., *Sex and Danger in Buenos Aires: Prostitution, Family and Nation in Argentina* (Lincoln, NE, 1991)

Historia del tango, La, 19 vols (Buenos Aires, 1976–87)

Hodges, Donald, *Argentina, 1943–1976* (Albuquerque, NM, 1976)

James, Daniel, 'Perón and the people' in *The Argentina Reader: History, Culture, Politics, ed.* G. Nouzielles and Gabriela Montaldo (Durham, NC, 2002)

Kassabova, Kapka, *Twelve Minutes of Love: A Tango Story* (London, 2011)

Keeling, David, J., *Buenos Aires: Global Dreams, Local Crises* (Chichester, 1996)

Kukkonen, Pirjo, *Tango Nostalgia: The Language of Love and Longing* (Helsinki, 1996)

Kutri, Carlos, *Piazzolla: la música límite* (Buenos Aires, 1992)

Legido, Juan Carlos, *La orilla oriental del tango: historia del tango uruguayo* (Montevideo, 1994)

Matamoro, Blas, *El Tango* (Madrid, 1996)

Munck, Ronaldo, *Argentina, from Anarchism to Peronism: Workers, Unions and Politics, 1855–1985* (London, 1987)

Pellicoro, Paul, *On Tango* (London, 2002)

Piazzolla, Diana, *Astor* (Buenos Aires, 1987)

Puccia, Enrique, H., *El Buenos Aires de Angel Villoldo* (Buenos Aires, 1976)

Rock, David, *Argentina, 1516–1987* (London, 1987)

——, *Politics in Argentina, 1890–1930: The Rise and Fall of Radicalism* (Cambridge, 1975)

Romano, Eduardo, *Las letras del tango: antología cronológica, 1900–1980* (Rosario, 1991)

Romero, Migdalia, *Tango Lover's Guide to Buenos Aires: Insights and Recommendations* (Bloomington, IN, 2009)

Sábato, Ernesto, *Tango, discusión y clave* (Buenos Aires, 1963)

Salas, Horacio, *El tango* (Buenos Aires, 1986)

Salmon, Russell O., 'The Tango: Its Origins and Meaning', *Journal of Popular Culture,* x/45 (1977), pp. 859–66

Savigliano, Marta E., *Tango and the Political Economy of Passion* (Boulder, CA, 1995)

Scobie, James, *Buenos Aires: Plaza to Suburb, 1870–1910* (New York, 1974)

Storm Roberts, John, *The Latin Tinge* (New York, 1999)

Taylor, Julie, *Paper Tangos* (Durham, NC, 2003)

——, 'Tango: Themes of Class and Nation', *Ethnomusicology,* xx/2 (May 1976), pp. 273–91

Turner, David, *A Passion for Tango* (Dingley, 2006)

Vardero, Arcángel Pascual, *El tango en la década de los 50* (California, 2011)

Watter, Richard, J., *Politics and Urban Growth in Buenos Aires, 1910–42* (Cambridge, 1993)

Wilson, Jason, *Buenos Aires: A Cultural and Literary Companion* (Oxford, 1999)

Winter, Brian, *Long After Midnight at the Niño Bien: The Tango and Argentina* (London, 2008)

Zumballaga, C., *Gardel* (Madrid, 1976)

DISCOGRAPHY AND FILMOGRAPHY

DISCOGRAPHY

There are close to 9,000 CDs of tango music currently available, so this is a tiny selection. We have tried to offer a representative sample as the basis for a collection.

Rough Guide to Tango, various artists, 2009, Proper, 1906063435, two-disc set
Rough Guide to Tango Nuevo, various artists, 2008, Proper, B0002LQUBK
Astor Piazolla The Soul of Tango: Greatest Hits, 2000, Milan Records, B00004NHEK
Astor Piazzolla, Jorge Calandrelli, Yo-Yo Ma, Antonio Agri, *Piazolla: Soul of the Tango*, 1997, Classical, B0000267PD
Astor Piazzolla and the Kronos Quartet, *Piazolla: Five Tango Sensations*, 1991, Nonesuch, B000005JOM
Adriana Varela, *Vuelve el Tango*, 2004, Nuevos Medios, B0000283HP
Mi Buenos Aires Querido, Carlos Gardel, Astor Piazzolla, Alberto Giunastera and Horacio Salgan, 1996, Teldec, B000000S97
Antologia Noble del Tango, 2006, Yoyousa, B0014RRDZ1, 6 discs
Aníbal Troilo, *Tango – Completes*, 2003, Magenta, B004213GSG, 2 discs
Glorias del Tango Series 1: Carlos Di Sarli, 2003, Selasco, B000VBDVIS
The Best of Carlos Gardel, 1998, EMI, B0000006Q60
Carlos Gardel, *Buenos Aires Tangos*, Music Brokers, 2008, B001AE3VIU
Le Tango à Paris 1907–1941, various artists, 1999, Frémeaux & Asssociés, B000027YA5
Los Grandes del Tango, Astor Piazzolla, Osvaldo Fresedo, Francisco Canaro, Miguel Calo, Florinda Sassone, Aníbal Troilo, Alfredo Gobbi, Juan D'Arienzo, Julio de Caro
Tango Argentino (The Original Cast Recording), 1999, Atlantic, B0000021JO
Bajofondo Tango Club, 2004, Commercial Marketing, B0000AKPNN
Tanghetto, *Hybrid Tango*, 2004, Constitution Music, B0009SQ430
Gotan Project, *La Revancha del Tango*, 2001, XL, B00005QZH2
The Beginners Guide to Tango, 2004, Nascente, NSBOX 010, 3 discs
Buenos Aires Tango Lunfardo, 2008, Music Brokers, B001AI7K68

Susana Rinaldi, *Milonga por Tantas Cosas*, 2005, Musicrama / Koch, B000A2X6H2
Los Grandes Clasicos Del Tango: Astor Piazzolla, 2001, Blue Moon, B000058E46

FILMOGRAPHY

Tango Bar, dir. John Reinhardt, USA, 1936

Last Tango in Paris, dir. Bernardo Bertolucci, France / Italy, 1973

El Exilio de Gardel (Tangos) dir. Fernando Solanas, France / Argentina, 1986

Tango Bar, dir. Marcos Zurinaga, Argentina / Puerto Rico, 1988

Sur, dir. Fernando Solanas, France / Argentina, 1990

Naked Tango, dir. Leonard Schrader, Switzerland / Argentina / Japan / USA, 1991

Tango, dir. Patrice Leconte, France, 1993

Scent of a Woman, dir. Martin Brest, USA, 1993

The Tango Lesson, dir. Sally Potter, UK / France / Argentina / Germany / Netherlands, 1997

Tango, dir. Carlos Saura, Spain / Argentina, 1999

Assassination Tango, dir. Robert Duvall, USA / Argentina, 2002

The Tango Dancer, dir. Francis Xavier, USA, 2006

Valentina's Tango, dir. Rogelio Lobato, USA, 2007

El café de los maestros, dir. Miguel Kohan, USA / Brazil / UK / Argentina, 2008
    (documentary)

ACKNOWLEDGEMENTS

Our thanks for their help and support go to Gerardo Ballesteros, Galo Cerón, Paddy Cunneen, Ricardo y Jenny in Edinburgh, Shona and Alistair in Glasgow, Norma and José in Buenos Aires, Lourdes (Lula) Contreras, Néstor Tarasona in Mérida and very special thanks to Carlos Rivodó.

COPYRIGHT ACKNOWLEDGEMENTS

INDEX

The Reverb series looks at the connections between music, artists and performers, musical cultures and places. It explores how our cultural and historical understanding of times and places may help us to appreciate a wide variety of music, and vice versa.

reverb-series.co.uk
Series editor: John Scanlan

Already published

The Beatles in Hamburg
Ian Inglis

Van Halen: Exuberant California, Zen Rock'n'Roll
John Scanlan

Brazilian Jive: From Samba to Bossa and Rap
David Treece

Tango: Sex and Rhythm of the City
Mike Gonzales and Marianella Yanes

TANGO